Scream Quietly
or the
Neighbours will Hear

Erin Pizzey

Edited by Alison Forbes

Penguin Books

Penguin Books Ltd, Harmondsworth, Middlesex, England
Penguin Books Inc., 7110 Ambassador Road, Baltimore, Maryland 21207, U.S.A.
Penguin Books Australia Ltd, Ringwood, Victoria, Australia
Penguin Books Canada Ltd, 41 Steelcase Road West, Markham, Ontario, Canada
Penguin Books (N.Z.) Ltd, 182–190 Wairau Road, Auckland 10, New Zealand

—

First published 1974

—

Copyright © Erin Pizzey, 1974

—

Made and printed in Great Britain
by C. Nicholls & Company Ltd
Set in Monotype Plantin

Acknowledgements

To the mothers and children who have contributed to this book, and to Margaret Hofmann who typed it.

I would also like to thank Jack Ashley, Neville Vincent and John Pontin for giving the mothers and children a future and Dr John Gayford who is carrying out research on battered wives.

Contents

Chapter 1

A House for Women

IN 1971 a small group of women came together in Chiswick to do something about rising prices on our high road. We decided to stand in the street on Saturdays with placards giving the prices of staple foods at each store. This campaign was quite a success: there was evidence of genuine price-cutting among some of the stores. As we stood on the street corners, we met lots of young mothers who all complained about the same thing – isolation. They felt cut off in their homes. This is really what set Women's Aid in motion: I formed the idea of a community centre where women and their children could come to meet and escape, for a time, from loneliness.

Though I was the only person in the group who was a feminist, all of us felt that the publicity that surrounded the Women's Lib movement put many women off. Centres like ours could be a positive step to getting women together outside their homes so that they could talk about the things they found unacceptable and set about changing them.

I wrote several letters to the local council, got the support of one of the local papers – the *Brentford and Chiswick Times* – and soon the Borough of Hounslow gave us the keys of a small house in Belmont Terrace. The house had been derelict for six years and was due to be demolished. As I type this, it is in ruins. There was no money at all, but a local bank was persuaded to give us an overdraft, and we set to. Luckily there was a rare man to help us. Most builders are pessimists but Harry Ferrer cheerfully took on all the jobs that were difficult for us and refrained from male chauvinist remarks when we put hinges on the wrong way round and drove rawlplugs into electric cables. Within eight weeks the crumbling condemned house was turned into a comfortable base.

9

Many women heard about the little house and came round to help. We made our first priority the play area, so that mothers with small children would be able to join in the decorating without fearing for them or feeling they were in the way. We put a cooker and a sink unit in the scullery and some kind man brought round a huge old Thor washing machine, which was a blessing. Upstairs had two rooms. One was the office and the other had a bed in it for emergencies. A year later there were thirty-four women and children living in the community: I wonder, if we'd known what was to happen, whether we might not have put down our paint-brushes and run.

The house opened without any ceremony – we were all too exhausted, and everything we owned was covered in orange paint, for the children had joined in the painting. After long discussions we called the house Chiswick Women's Aid. One of the more artistic members did a sign for the front door and we were in business.

One of the few rules we had was that the house belonged to all women. Any woman who wished could get a key cut and keep it. Men were only allowed in by invitation. This seemingly practical rule aroused the most amazing hostility from men. In vain we pointed out that we accepted that they all had clubs, pubs and sporting events that excluded women, so why should our gesture cause so much hostility? It did, but the rule stayed.

At the back of 2, Belmont Terrace were rows and rows of small houses, all due to be demolished. Some were being used by the borough for temporary housing, because the housing situation was at crisis point. Conditions were dreadful. There were rats, leaking walls, no bathrooms, outside lavatories and no hot water. Most of the women in these houses lived on their own with children – widowed, divorced, unmarried, or with husbands in jail. Social security gives just enough to survive on, not enough to live. All of us collected material from places like the Claimants' Union and the Citizen's Rights Office and sat down to absorb the baffling rules and regulations that govern 'the welfare'. We soon became experts on the rights of mothers and children.

Before long we came up against some very prickly social workers who felt we were interfering. Not all of them were hostile. Very few of the women objected – it was mainly the men. They found it difficult to accept that women whom they considered inadequate should ring them up quoting chapter and verse from handbooks that they didn't know existed. Besides, when social workers called at Chiswick Women's Aid they expected to find someone in authority, i.e. a labelled person like a chairwoman or treasurer, to be sitting behind the desk, not the woman who was their 'client'.

Few of the people who came to the centre had money to spare, but many had old clothes, so we raised money jumbling. Some mothers would say they had come to buy second-hand clothes and then stay and ask for help with the endless round of trying to survive. We kept coal fires going so that everyone would be warm, at least during the day. We shared massive stews and soups and the washing machine was churning all day because on social security launderettes can be out of your reach.

Indira was one of the first women to come in and make herself at home. A qualified teacher, and of the highest caste, she had flown to England to look for a post as headmistress of one of our better-known schools. She came to us to talk about her accommodation problem. Her landlady was no lady and she would have to move yet again. I've rarely met anyone as resourceful as Indira. Immigration regulations, the need for a job or a place to live . . . whatever her problem she always found a way through. She is one of the world's survivors.

The first woman to stay at the centre was utterly different. Jill was a wraith-like figure who seemed to be totally homeless and friendless. She had been in and out of hospitals because she couldn't absorb food. When she'd come out this time her landlady wanted to put up the rent and she couldn't pay the increase, so she'd nowhere to go. It seemed quite simple; a roof for a week or two and a helping hand in finding another room and a good job. We did not doubt that she could get a good job – she had a degree. Until we collected her trunk from her old landlady we found some excellent cast-offs from the heap we had piled up for the day of the great jumble sale.

In the centre Jill was tremendous – she ran the office and answered the phone and listened for hours to other people's problems. She was always sweet and gentle and dignified. Weeks went by and funds were at an all-time low, so we hired a hall for the jumble sale. It was a posh hall in an expensive district. We were very pleased. Indira announced that she could not possibly soil her hands with second-hand clothes. Daddy would not hear of her doing such a thing. Yet as the piles of clothing grew higher we noticed that an awful lot of the good stuff was going. Sure enough Indira was discovered making for the door with a big bundle stuffed under her coat. We took her upstairs, sorted out a magnificent array of clothing and pressed it into her arms, explaining that jumble was practically a British way of life.

Jill was put in charge of organizing the hall at 10 a.m. and the mountains of clothes were all priced. I arrived at the hall at 10.30 to find the vicar standing on the doorstep looking very unchristian. 'Your helper,' he said, breathing laboriously, 'is drunk.' I was absolutely furious with him. I knew that Jill never drank alcohol – even if we all shared a bottle of wine she would stick to orange juice. I went in. There was Jill lurching around the hall looking like death. She had fallen badly and blood was dripping from her head. I didn't think she was drunk because she certainly didn't smell of drink. I led her out and drove her to the casualty department. They took her in and I said I'd call back that evening.

The jumble sale was exhausting. It was the first of many that we have had to run to keep our heads above water. The work is enormous and the rewards small, but it is the only way to get bills paid if you have no other form of income. The £70 we made seemed like a fortune then.

I went back to the hospital and asked them what had caused the dreadful lurching. In other words, 'Had she been drunk?'

'No,' said the doctor, 'certainly not. It was concussion from the fall.' I took her back to the centre.

Jill was thrilled when she was offered a room in return for baby-sitting and she quickly settled in with a family. The children, who were eight and nine, seemed to get on very well with her, and their mother was so pleased that she decided to go on a short holiday. On the Saturday one of the children came running to my house, his face white with fear. Something had happened to Jill.

I rushed round. There, on the sitting-room floor, crawling

on her hands and knees, whining like a dog, was Jill. She had wet herself and she was mumbling. The little girl was huddled in a corner, crying. I put my arms round Jill and said, 'Why didn't you tell me?' because this time there was no mistaking the smell of alcohol.

'Go away,' she mumbled, 'I'll be all right in a minute.' She rose wobbling to her feet and then collapsed onto her back.

'You're an alcoholic,' I said.

'I'm not, I'm not. I'm ill.' She became very angry and tried to order me out of the house. I wouldn't leave because of the children. Finally she stopped shouting at me, put her hands over her face and screamed.

'Yes! Yes! Won't you go away . . . Yes, I drink.' Then she collapsed and passed out.

I got her to bed. Her room was full of bottles. Bottles of sherry. Jill only drank sherry and that only out of sherry glasses. I called in a friend who was able to stay the night with the children and the next morning Jill and I sat down and talked.

Jill had been the darling of her father and had a brilliant future mapped out for her. The other members of the family did well and Jill got her degree. However, in her concept of woman's role, marriage was the ultimate goal beyond any other achievement, so when her engagement to a peer of the realm which crowned her successful life came to nothing, Jill felt a complete failure. She had been an alcoholic for years. She was well known to one hospital but she often found herself in others after a particularly bad bout of drinking. She had never before admitted to herself, let alone to anyone else, that she drank. The hospitals treated her for malabsorption because they never realized that she was living entirely on alcohol and that by this time she did indeed have a problem of malabsorption because she rarely ate anything.

It was the first time I'd come across an alcoholic. I could see how hard it can be to detect the problem if the person disguises it as well as Jill did. Jill decided to go back into the one hospital that was home to her to see if she could get dried out. She visits us from time to time but the hospital do not feel that there is much hope for her because the life she was brought up to expect was hers by right folded under her, and the real world is a very harsh place for a princess, so they expect her to drink her way out of it.

It was about this time that a young girl called Jenny came into the centre and asked for help for her mother and father who were both in hospital with overdoses. She told us about life in her family.

About nine years before, Jenny's dad, Bert, had an accident at work which involved severe head injuries. During the time he was in hospital her mum, Sue, was looking after five children (aged seven to fifteen), keeping her home and her two jobs. She went on working because she simply didn't realize that she might be entitled to social security benefits, nor did anyone at the hospital tell her. Also Bert had no compensation money from his employers, although he'd worked for them for more than fifteen years: shortly after his accident they sent him notice and one week's pay.

After about four weeks, Bert was discharged from hospital, though he still went to out-patient sessions. Sue began to get desperate: Bert was always weeping and shaking and wringing his hands. He used to get extremely agitated if he was kept in a confined place for very long. He tried to find work, but couldn't hold any job for long because of his claustrophobia. Obviously the strain was too much for Sue and gradually she found consolation in taking one of the sleeping tablets Bert had brought home with him. Then she got 100 Mandrax tablets on prescription from her doctor. She began taking three or four tablets a night and was in a hell of a state, but she wasn't yet addicted. Three years or so went by and by this time Sue was so desperate that she went back to the hospital to ask if they could improve Bert's condition. They offered to do a brain operation – leucotomy – warning her that it hadn't even a fifty–fifty chance of success, as not many of them had been done before. The operation was a success, as far as Sue was told. Bert was like a child, which they said was quite normal. Sue was really upset by the effect on Bert and by now was so heavily doped most of the time that the three eldest children left home. The two youngest (boys) began to get into trouble with the police. One was put on probation.

When Bert had 'grown up' again, the hospital sent him home, presumably well. But, though the hospital hadn't mentioned it, Bert had developed a streak of violence since his operation. He took to beating Sue viciously when they were alone. By this stage Sue was in and out of the psychiatric and general hospitals, each time because she'd taken an overdose to get away from his beatings. Nobody did anything to help her between the overdoses. One time, when she was heavily drugged, he hit her and cut her head open. The hospital treated the wound only. They stitched it up and sent her home. Bert said she had fallen.

Once when Jenny called to see her father she found him in tears. He was frantic. He and Sue had had a fight in the morning and she had left home with a suitcase. She did come back that night but she was drugged to the hilt and collapsed on the floor. Jenny and Bert made her vomit and tried to revive her. She was taken to West Middlesex, transferred to Springfield, took an overdose of aspirin there and was pumped out at St George's and returned to Springfield. The day after she was discharged she was drugged again. She'd been to Piccadilly again and collapsed on the doorstep at three in the afternoon. The doctor said to ring 999. The emergency service said to ring the doctor.

In the end an ambulance took her to the general hospital. Here is the situation as Jenny wrote it down:

Dad was in such a state it was impossible for him to go anywhere and all of us were rallying round him as he needed support. Alan [Jenny's husband] and I called that same night to Mum's ward and the nurse said she may be coming home Wednesday. I accepted this and then went home. On the Tuesday I telephoned to say Dad could not have Mum home as he was on night work and this meant there would be no one to receive her. It was deferred until Friday. In between this Miss Taylor the social worker telephoned on behalf of Mum to the next-door neighbour to ask for her clothes and cigarettes and money. My sister took the call and said she would bring these things but not the money. The social worker got irate and friction developed. By then Dad begged me to get help. I saw a neighbour who advised us to see a legal-aid adviser and if possible our MP. I managed to get in touch on the Thursday morning. Prior to this I rang the GP and asked for an appointment. I was told he did not make appointments, I would have to wait in line with his patients and if he was free he'd see me. Not satisfied, I rang the physician, Dr

Simpson, and begged him to help Mum because of a threat Dad made if she was let out they would take an overdose to kill them both. He said he knew he could not help her and that the only way I could help, which I suggested, was in fact to see if the police could find her selling or buying drugs. This of course was not acceptable so I asked could she not be sent to a cure ward, i.e. Shenley, St Bernards. He said there is no cure. I pleaded for help. He said he could give no further help. This was Wednesday. I contacted our local M P and made arrangements for him to talk to me. I explained the situation and he said he would try and help. I rang at 10 p.m. that evening and he told me that he had rung and that he would be ringing again tomorrow.

I decided to spend the night at Dad's, as I knew he had seen the state of Mum and he thought she was dying. We got to his home and we talked and had tea. Suddenly he collapsed. I called for my brothers to help Alan. We thought he had taken an overdose and we took him off to the hospital in Alan's van but Dad became worse and stopped breathing. My brother tried mouth-to-mouth respiration but it was no good. Alan saw two ambulance men and got an ambulance to the van. He was taken to the hospital from there. Tim and John waited, they admitted him and after a stomach pump they were told he would be O K. At 1.30 that night I went to the hospital to make sure and they said, 'He is O K. He will probably be discharged tomorrow.'

Both parents were discharged but within a few days the mother was back in the hospital with yet another attempt at suicide. I visited her with Jenny and it was obvious that the staff treated her with utter contempt as a junkie who was taking up a bed needed for a sick person. Sue was wrapped in a hospital dressing-gown. She looked tiny and wizened and was lurching and stumbling, as the effects of the pills had not yet worn off. She cried pathetically and begged me for help. I said cheerfully we should be able to find some unit who would take her and help her get off the pills, but I discovered that nobody wants a middle-aged drug addict. They are considered a bad risk and not worth the effort, and nowhere could I get anybody to offer us accommodation for Sue.

Out again, Sue began to come to the centre and during the hours of talking she told us of the scenes of violence that occurred when Bert lost his temper. Up to that time she hadn't told anyone what was happening. For a while even the children hadn't known.

One day she seemed very disorientated. She showed us terrible bruising on her body. We contacted our local social services who said there was nothing they could do, but they promised to visit Bert. He refused to let them into the house. The social workers said it was one of the worst cases in Hounslow. The police, too, had often been called to the house.

Eventually Bert became more openly violent and took to attacking Sue in front of the boys. On the day that Bert was stabbed I visited their house. In his rage he had totally destroyed the banisters and the furniture and was breaking through the party wall with a hammer when the neighbours called the police. They were too late: he had lifted up a washing machine to throw it at his wife when the older boy picked up a knife and stabbed him in the stomach. His blood was splattered up the walls.

By now Sue was almost beyond despair. It was heartbreaking to see her. Bert was in hospital seriously ill, but there was a chance he might survive to live in a wheelchair or walk with a tripod.

We decided to write to the Secretary of State for Health and Social Security, Sir Keith Joseph. We described the series of misfortunes Sue and Bert had suffered and asked the Minister if he could do anything to resolve their problems, as it appeared that the professional welfare and social services agencies had, even with the best of intentions, failed to give them the comfort and support they needed.

Within ten days we were invited to attend a case conference at West Middlesex Hospital. It all sounded very grand. Three of us went. There were about ten people in the room including people from the local social services and the psychiatrist. They seemed rather disturbed that we had written to the Minister. We pointed out that with all the sympathy and goodwill in the world this family was continually in a crisis situation. All everybody seemed to do was to patch up their wounds and send them back into the arena.

The hospital then put forward their case. They said they were sincerely sorry about the ill-effects of the operation and they quite agreed that the family had slipped through the net of their medical social workers. However, there was nothing that could be done, for though the man should be committed, he was guilty of no crime that justified committing him.

'Except,' we pointed out, 'repeated violent attacks against his wife.'

'Oh yes, that,' was the dismissive answer.

Hospitals, doctors, psychiatrists, social workers, police, all the people one had imagined were there to care – not one of them seemed to be bothered that this woman was being beaten regularly by a man who was the victim of an operation that had gone hideously wrong.

Sue lived in the centre with us while Bert was in hospital. Jill was marvellous to her – she listened for hours and helped her when she was too stoned to cope. We tried to help her stay off pills but she'd been through too many years, years of hard work and misery with the dreadful strain of trying to keep going. In the back of her mind she knew that whatever her husband had done to her, the fault was outside his control, so that when he came out of hospital she went back to him and they tried to make life bearable for each other.

When the time came for the son to stand trial for attempted murder we had to subpoena the psychiatrist because he resisted a polite request to give evidence. However, he told the court that the aggression was due to the operation and the head injuries and not the man's fault. After more details of the way that the family, and particularly the children, had been forced to live, the case was cut short by the prosecution and the judge directed the jury to find the boy 'not guilty'. Yet, before he was released on bail, that young boy had spent six months in remand, many hours in solitary confinement and would carry a scar round with him for the rest of his life.

This family's tragedy only occurred because of an indifferent and uncaring system of looking after people. Sue's case was the first time we had become deeply involved in the problem of violence in the family. Once people heard about what we had been doing for her they began to knock on the door and ask for help.

Apart from the women like Sue and Jill who came in and stayed, there were several who dropped by regularly, like Mrs Murphy who lived down the back and suffered from agoraphobia. Someone from her street had walked her round to us to have a cup of coffee and a look through some of the clothes. She was a lovely, jolly lady who had brought up nine children. One day the subject of wife-bashing was being discussed and she suddenly put down her cup and said:

'My husband's beaten me all our married life.'

It had started nineteen years before, when she was pregnant with the first child and he took up with another woman. When he came home from the pub or from his job in a bad mood he just laid into her. The last time he beat her he took her by the shoulders and banged her head against the wall in the passage until she was unconscious, and then pushed her head under the cold tap in the scullery until she came round, and then banged her head against the wall again.

'Why didn't you leave him?' I asked, not thinking.

'Where do I go with the children? . . .'

'What about the social services?'

'They just told me to go home.'

At this point we decided to check this out and we telephoned all the surrounding boroughs, including our own. They all pointed out that a woman who leaves home has voluntarily made herself homeless and therefore is not entitled to any assistance from social services. All they would offer her was a visit from a social worker. We'd seen how useless that was to Sue. Besides, in the case of a wife who is badly beaten a social worker's visit is too dangerous because it can be used to justify another beating. So the mothers usually go back home and put up with it again until next time. 'It is not,' the particularly pompous social worker told me, 'the policy of the social services to interfere with the sanctity of marriage.'

About this time we had a mother in with a young child. Brenda's husband had beaten her very badly and she was covered with bruises; both her eyes were black. Her small daughter, who was four, had a huge bruise on her cheek. I thought it would be a good idea to take them both to hospital for a check-up. The doctor at the casualty department merely noted the mother's bruises and then wrote down on the child's records, 'Mother claims father hit child.' So much for battered babies.

Brenda stayed with us for some time and then moved in with her parents. She took a course in social work and as far as I know is happily settled. Her husband is a manic depressive. He is still refusing the psychiatric treatment he so badly needs and is unemployable, but at least his small daughter no longer has to witness her mother being beaten and raped.

Not long after that, a middle-class mother arrived at the door with four children. She said she had read about us in the *Guardian* and had always meant to come round to help but never in her wildest dreams had she considered that she might have to come for refuge. Her husband – a company director – had been violent for quite a while but she had always put up with it. She walked out because he had tried to throttle the eldest child. I was beginning to realize that quite a lot of women will put up with unimaginable cruelty to themselves but once the man attacks the children they leave for good. So she too settled in at Belmont Terrace.

At about this time Anne Ashby joined me. I was in the local park at a 1 o'clock club with my goddaughter Rachael. I saw a small, plump woman sitting by herself on a bench and I walked over and introduced myself to her. She had been a nurse and had had a varied career so I asked her what she did all day now. She said, 'Nothing much.' So that solved that and she came down to Belmont Terrace for a look at the place and is now worked to death and invaluable to everybody.

As a result of radio and television broadcasts and newspaper reports our name was getting known nationally. Every piece of publicity brought more cries for help. Letters were arriving from all over the country:

Dear Mrs Pizzey,

I am wondering if you could help me as I'm in a rather difficult situation. I live in Bradford and have six children between thirteen and three years old and I have a very unhappy home life.

My husband is a very violent man and is very hard to reason with. He keeps me very short of money even though he has a good wage at — Bradford. Sometimes he's very violent to me. On one occasion I had to run out of the house at midnight and go to a friend's house to call the police. I suffer very badly with my nerves and at forty I don't think I can have this strain on me much more. I was living in Clapham for four years but came to Bradford to live to see if I could get more help here.

I have been to the welfare, family advice and have a solicitor but nobody seems really interested in my case. Even the Samaritans.

I have left my husband in desperation five times but have had to return for my children's sake, as he didn't take care of them in my absence.

At the moment we are living in a council house which is in his name. He keeps telling me to go and sometimes says, 'Take the children,' and other times says, 'Leave them.'

He treats me like a dog and at the moment I am having strong nerve drugs from my doctor but still can't rest as he's continually picking on me and the children.

Being as the children are growing up, especially the first three of thirteen, twelve and eleven, they witness some terrible scenes and it is making them ill and backward in their lessons at school. They cry and cling to me and try to shelter me when he's hitting me or making sexual demands so I'm wondering if you could see me and help me, please. Sometimes I feel like committing suicide and taking the children with me. I must get help from somewhere but no one helps me or wants to know. Please don't send any correspondence here as my husband can read them and will kill me if he gets to know, so please send any letters care of — and they will pass it to me secretly. I do so need help. I am really desperate and before long will be in an asylum. I need a divorce but can't get one because I don't want to leave my children with this monster as he is cruel to them. If you could help me, could you send an appointment and directions of how to get to you in London.

Yours truly,

London

Dear Mrs Pizzey,

I read your article yesterday and thought you might be interested in my case.

I was a beaten-up wife and stood it for twenty-four years. I finally left in December 1971 and obtained my divorce for persistent cruelty in September 1972. I left a three-bedroomed maisonette (council) and am now classed as a homeless family.

The council gave me temporary accommodation in this patch repair house. Soon I hope something better will turn up. I have three boys: one is married (twenty-three years), one aged fourteen years is with me, and the other, aged eighteen, is still living with his father, the reason

21

being I have only one bedroom and it would be too crowded with all of us.

I have left everything: my home, much of which I bought, as my ex-husband had no interest in the home and I went to work part-time for the last eight years of my marriage. I did all the decorating, everything, and yet he has gained everything, even though it was all his fault.

Something should be done to allow a wife (the innocent party) to claim at least half of everything. Why after all should the husband keep the tenancy of the marital home, where the wife is in need? All I have now has been given to me by family and friends. I had nothing. Even my son (who is not with me) has to suffer because he misses me and would rather be with me, but cannot because I have no room while my ex-husband lives in comfort in a three-bedroomed maisonette.

That is the law and I think you are doing something worth while if you could change the law.

Good luck to you,

Yours sincerely,

Yorkshire

Dear Mrs Pizzey,

I saw the item in today's *Sun*, about you trying to get a commission set up to look into wife-beating and obtain a change in the law.

I couldn't agree more. Nearly two years ago I married a man who turned out to be violent. Before this I had never encountered personal violence. I had no idea what hell on earth was like. My husband beat me up constantly whilst I was pregnant with our son Simon, now aged fourteen months. He kicked me, stood on me, punched me and throttled me into insensibility time and again. I don't know if this was the cause but our child was born blind and mentally retarded. Even though my husband is now in prison – not for beating me, oh no, he is much too clever to be caught for that – I live in fear of him. I dread the time when he will be released.

I have discussed all this in greater detail with the doctors and specialists who have been examining Simon. They all agree that my husband has a personality handicap, he has a split personality, he is an aggressive psychotic and incurable – also, however, it is not a mental condition for which he can be institutionalized. I have spoken to his solicitor who knows his bad record for violence and he says until he actually kills me, or seriously injures me – or someone else – nothing can be done.

The prison welfare officers admit that once he has served his sentence he will be unconditionally released (about July). I have spoken to other welfare officers, the Samaritans, everyone I can think of and I can find no hope or help anywhere. Everyone says it seems incredible. I have a daughter of five by a previous marriage (her father is dead) and the handicapped little boy to bring up – do I have to spend the rest of my life hiding and living in fear, afraid to let them out of my sight, afraid to be anywhere on my own, in case he comes after me?

I am absolutely desperate and I am not an ignorant teenager. I am in my forties, intelligent and well educated. I read so many cases in the papers now, where, reading between the lines, I realize there are many other women in a similar situation to myself.

I am sick of people telling me nothing can be done, it is incredible that one person can treat another so diabolically. He smashed my big toe with a hammer one night and I didn't dare tell the hospital the truth in case he got off with a fine or conditional discharge and was free to exact retribution.

I see three women M Ps are supporting your efforts. I'm sure more publicity should be given to this, it is vital, it affects children terribly too.

I bet the woman official of the Marriage Guidance Council who said, 'It is not always the man who is to blame,' has never been smashed to the ground time and time again by her husband's fist or anything he can lay his hands on in her own living room.

If there is anything I can do to help your cause, or anything you can do to help me, please contact me but for heaven's sake don't publish my name – they get newspapers in prison.

Yours very sincerely,

Women of all areas, classes and races were crying out for help as soon as they knew there was somebody who would listen and could do something to help them.

Some, like Kath, just came. Kath was very frightened. She'd been married and beaten for seven years. Her husband had beaten her up the previous week and then laid into her again that day. Afterwards he told her to get out or be killed. She left that night, travelled to London with her three children and telephoned us from Victoria Station the next morning.

For every woman who contacted us on her own initiative, just as many were referred to us by the endless agencies who can give advice, but don't offer shelter: Citizens' Advice Bureaux, probation officers, the Samaritans, doctors, magistrates and social workers.

Some of the social workers – the caring ones – brought their clients to us. Others would ring us to say how worried they were about their clients and how they would send them back home to a certain beating if we didn't take them. A house vote would be taken, another mattress found and we'd make the family welcome. Some social services were at least open about their reliance on us: Islington used to put their families in a taxi and pay the fare to Chiswick.

It's not, as popularly supposed, only the Andy Capps who oppress their wives with violence; some so-called gentlemen are hardly gentle. It's just as much engineers and welders, executives and lorry drivers, dentists and mechanics, general practitioners and labourers. I sometimes think it's a pity that only a few of the middle-class women who come through our doors will allow themselves to be quoted. If they all did we would see a change overnight because it is their husbands, the civil servants, judges, doctors, solicitors and councillors, who can do most to alleviate the situation all women are in. What is more, from the way the police generally react to appeals for help from assaulted wives, it doesn't surprise me that quite a few policemen's wives ask for our help.

It's all races too. One social worker we came across informed Women's Aid that wife-beating was a West Indian syndrome. He hadn't received and hadn't expected complaints from women of any other group. The reaction of the women in the house was, 'Paint yourselves black, girls!'

We've always maintained we are ready to cooperate with anyone who is willing to help. We could soon see that the demand for help outstripped our resources, but the idea was already spreading. More and more groups of women were coming – from Guildford, Croydon, Southend, Canterbury, Manchester – to see us and find out what we were doing and how we went about it. Some groups we considered publicity-seekers, and the house decision was that we should not support them. Unfortunately, when a new idea begins to bear fruit some people wish to use it for their own ends. The community has a good nose for this sort of thing and they soon slip away with nothing accomplished.

But for the few groups that are no good there are many others. They go back to talk to their friends in their own areas and begin to set up refuges themselves. About thirty-eight groups from all over Britain, with one from Dublin, came to a conference in April 1974. Some are already operating. By the end of the year many more will have opened house.

The problem does not belong to Britain alone. We have had reporters to the house from Denmark, Switzerland, Canada and Germany and several from the United States. Articles were published in Italy and Sweden too. A Dutch crew made a short film for television which was put out at peak viewing time in Holland. When it finished the studio switchboard was crammed with telephone calls, most of them saying, 'Why show British women in this predicament? What about us?'

Chapter 2

A Man's Home
is his Castle

VIOLENCE in the streets – straight thuggery and mugging – is treated as a serious crime. The normal sentences are ten to fifteen years for grievous bodily harm. The victims get full cooperation from the police. Newspapers give front-page cover. Mugging is universally deplored.

If the same act is committed behind the front door it is ignored. The following account will give some idea of the way the agents of society – doctors, social workers, housing department, solicitors, police and courts – can treat a woman who is viciously assaulted by her husband.

I was married in March 1964 at the age of sixteen. My husband, an undergraduate, was twenty-five. We were very happy until after the birth of the fourth child. By this time my husband had graduated, taken a job as a lecturer, given it up, started his own contracting business and was rapidly becoming a successful businessman. At first his drinking was restricted to weekends, then it became much more frequent, until by Christmas 1966 he was drinking every evening after work until long after midnight.

He would arrive home in a very drunken state and complain bitterly about everything I did or said to him. He was frightening when in this sort of aggressive mood but never made an attempt to hit me until 1969, on my son's fourth birthday. He arrived home at 9.30 p.m. and insisted I get James out of bed, in order to give him a present. After refusing, I eventually agreed to let him see James in the bedroom but he picked him up and brought him into the kitchen, where he was very insulting to me and called me a slut and a whore. I asked for an explanation; he told me he owed me nothing. I said I was about sick of this behaviour and wanted to put James back to bed. My husband refused to hand him over. James was crying and reaching out to me. I took James from my husband, he tried to get him back but James clung to me. After about three or four minutes my husband grabbed James and punched me behind my right ear at the same time. He picked up the bread-knife and threatened to put it through my throat. I told him I had taken my fill of him, threats, insults and now assaults. I said I was leaving and taking our children. His reply was that I could get out but if I tried to take the children he would kill me. I grabbed my coat and left the flat. I stayed the night in the convent where the children went to nursery school, collected them the following day and went home to my parents. I stayed away for nearly three weeks, during which time my husband visited us and asked me to return. After he gave me an undertaking never to touch me again, I went home. I was back seven months before the next assault.

During this time my husband was becoming increasingly possessive, stopping me from visiting my mother and godmother. He stopped me from communicating with all my past friends, saying that I should mix with married women. When I did this, he said my married friends were a bad influence on me – in fact every friend I have ever had was bad in his eyes. It occurs to me now that they were a threat to him; I had someone to turn to when he attacked me, also he may have been afraid that they would persuade me to leave him.

On this second assault, his friend came home with him at 3 a.m. I got up when told to because I feared another beating if I didn't. We sat and discussed music and politics for about an hour, when my husband suddenly began shouting at me and calling me names. I went to bed, when I was called back. I made a bed up for the guest. My husband suddenly accused me of flirting with his friend and 'fancying' him. I told him I never noticed another man from the day I became engaged to him. He called me a liar and hit me in the mouth. My top lip was split, and my mouth badly puffed and bruised. We went to bed and after refusing to have intercourse with my husband he hit me in the back of the head, causing my nose to spurt blood and tried to suffocate me with the pillow. I reported this assault to the hospital, because after the first incident I discovered that GPs don't want to know about husband-and-wife disputes and it is impossible to obtain a legal separation or divorce without some sort of medical evidence. Three days later, I returned from shopping to find all my clothes, including boots and shoes, ripped or slashed. My husband told me the children had mentioned a man being in hospital; he assumed I was having an affair with this person, who in fact was the brother of the woman who collected them from school. I had only the trousers I was wearing and had to ask my parents for money to buy clothes before I could return to college the following Monday.

After this he beat me regularly every four months, always after a drinking bout. Most of them were to my face and head, particularly my eyes; it is significant that from having perfect eyesight at sixteen, I now have great difficulty in reading the advertisements in the Tube. I tried to leave my husband. I contacted the Catholic Housing Aid Society, the Samaritans, the N S P C C, the housing department of the local authority. No one wanted to know. It was always the same. 'We can't give you somewhere to live because your husband can come back on us.' 'Obtain a separation and then we will help you.' There's only one problem here. The courts will not grant separation orders if the woman doesn't get out. They say: 'If the situation is as intolerable as you describe, how have you managed to stick it for this length of time?' It's one vicious circle of very large perimeter, with the woman in the middle and the husband and bureaucracy hitting out from all points.

On one occasion, after strapping my dislocated wrist, a sympathetic doctor advised me to contact social services. This I did as soon as the doors were open that Monday morning. I was told I must give my marriage a chance. I had been married for five and a half years at the time, so I thought the advice rather irrelevant. When I told the social worker this she got quite abrupt with me and said I could not be given temporary accommodation but they would send someone to see my husband. This was done, and after four abortive attempts the social worker finally got him at home. He was very nice to her at first, then ended up telling her to get out and mind her own business, and said he would look after the children if I left.

The next time I contacted this department was after my doctor had already rung them and impressed upon them that it was imperative that I be taken out of this situation. They told me to leave the children with my husband. He would look after them. I pointed out that three weeks before he had been placed on probation and had another assault case coming up the following week. I was told that if they felt he wouldn't care for the children (however, they had no evidence to this effect), they would be taken into care. All the children were being affected by this disturbing atmosphere, having witnessed almost every attack upon me, so I didn't think it would be wise to take the social worker's advice.

I realized that I would have to stick it out until I found an open door to a better life. I had saved over £500 and intended to get enough for a deposit on a house, when I returned to college. My husband found out about my savings and stopped giving me any money. I went through the money and then, when it was gone, gave up college and went to work. At this time I didn't know of the existence of social security.

Between 1969 and 1972 I had suffered twenty-seven brutal attacks, including ten which required me to be admitted to hospital for two days or more. Once I lost the baby I was expecting. The police came on all of these occasions and, while sympathetic, did nothing, except to tell me to take him to court. I was reluctant to do this, knowing he would attack me seriously, and maybe the result would be fatal. However, in the end I could stand it no more. After attempting to strangle me with our telephone wire he was charged by me and was bound over to keep the peace and fined £25. I had to pay this money out of my housekeeping money. Before this case got to court he came home drunk, tried to persuade me to drop the case, when I refused he got into a rage and beat me so much that he split my head open. He received a three-year probation period for this offence. He was given a suspended prison sentence when within a month he was in court again for grievous bodily harm. Two weeks after the latest court case my husband ripped my coat, kicked my pet terrier in the face and nearly broke my finger in an attempt to get my wedding ring, which he eventually bent and threw out of the window. These incidents took place on our eighth wedding anniversary. I left the following day. My husband tried to see me at my parents' home. He was let in twice and forced his way in another night. I was alone at home with my eighteen-year-old sister and the children. The police removed him and after he received another eight summonses he fled to Ireland. He was back in this country after one month, coming round frequently to our flat, which by this time I was occupying. After hitting me, trying to prevent me taking the children out and breaking down a door which fell onto my daughter's bed and narrowly missing her head, he moved into the flat, which I immediately left.

People say that the reason so many women suffer this sort of treatment is that women don't know their rights. Well, I knew mine. I informed my solicitor that I wanted to apply for an injunction. He agreed to do this, but first of all tried to tell me I had to move out. I proved to him that I had nowhere to go, then my husband left. He then said I had no need for an injunction. After I left finally in November 1972 I asked my solicitor to seek an injunction again. He said the court would take the view that I had somewhere to stay and would not grant the injunction. I took his word for it and now my husband has given up our flat. I am homeless and penniless with many scars both physical and mental to remind me of life with a jealous, alcoholic husband. However, I am happy again and know I will be able to rebuild the lives of my children and myself. I was lucky to be strong enough mentally to stick it out without breaking down completely, and fortunately my children don't seem to be suffering from their harrowing experiences.

Violence inside the home, within the family, is not new, and because it is not new, it is not easy to see it for what it is. People have had lots of practice in ignoring it. They will turn a blind eye or cross the road. They will even, as one woman told Women's Aid, turn up the TV to block out the shouting and sobbing next door so that they can no longer hear it.

Nobody usually wants to know about brutality within the family. There is a primitive mechanism in us all that makes us feel that misery is infectious. Those who fall foul of the broad path of success must therefore be kept away lest the bad luck transfer itself to the onlooker. The reason why I feel so strongly about it is that I know what it is like. I have been happily married for fourteen years and very rarely think about my child-hood, preferring to forget it, but when I am faced with a woman shaking with fear I know deep down exactly what she and her children feel and, possibly unlike most people she has approached, I am in a position to know that she isn't exaggerating.

When I first came into close contact with battered wives and mothers I found it alarming that things had not changed since I was a child. In fact they were getting worse. Families have been splitting up. The old convention was that as 'family' you did have a right to intervene. But now relations are sometimes hundreds of miles away. To strangers a man's home is his castle and that castle is not to be scaled by outsiders.

This myth must be re-examined and more humane ways discovered to give protection to the prisoners inside the castle, women and children. A man has always been able to get out of a miserable marriage because he always has the money and he rarely has the responsibility of the children. A woman usually has children and no money and nowhere to go. It is impossible to get rented accommodation on the open market if you have children. Landlords don't want to take on families because it is illegal to evict them.

People who are being ill-treated don't usually talk about it. Some are scared of what might happen to them if they speak. They know well that if they tell how they are treated they will again be threatened and most probably beaten. Many of the women who write to us ask for the reply to be sent care of friends or at their parents', because they are afraid they'll get another beating if their husbands find out that they've contacted us.

One woman just telephoned when her husband was out of the house and cried and sobbed. She was physically handicapped. Her husband, an alcoholic and a gambler, had put padlocks on the wheels of her chair. He would go off sometimes for several days at a time leaving her lying on the floor helpless. She never told us who she was. We would spend hours trying to convince her we could help, but she was too frightened of him.

Some keep silent out of loyalty and the wish to keep up appearances. They are ashamed to admit they are beaten and don't want to tell the neighbours. Several women were encouraged to write to us simply because radio and television programmes had shown them that many other women were in their predicament:

Dear Madam,

Please can you help me. My husband ill-treats me and I can no longer stand it. I have no one to turn to. I am alone except for my one-year-old son. My husband is given to violent tempers and my arms at times have been black and blue through his punches. He butted me on the nose two weeks ago and I had a terrible nose-bleed. Then in bed one night he started to strangle me and it was not until I passed out that he realized what he had done. For days it was hard for me to swallow. Up to now I have been too ashamed to go anywhere for help but after hearing yesterday's radio programme it gave me some courage to try and do something about my plight.

It is for my son's sake that I have wanted to keep the home together but now I feel it would be better for his well-being that we no longer remain in this environment. My husband shouts and breaks things in the house and frightens the baby. After my husband had knocked me on the floor one night the baby screamed in terror and I was hurt and too frightened to do anything. My husband now threatens to bash the baby's brains in. He swears I will never leave him. I've told him I want a divorce. Now I dare not say I want to go or he starts and I am afraid that either my life or my son's is in danger.

Last Christmas Eve when my husband had been hitting me I ran into the street and was on my way to the police station but he came after me and dragged me back and hit me again. Please help me. I begin to feel so ill. If it were not for my baby I would not bother you with my problems.

31

Last night for the first time I wondered how I might kill my husband in bed while he was asleep. This was after another show of violence because I refused his attentions. I do everything to keep the peace but I just cannot force myself to make love with him, it is all so hypocritical and I have absolutely no feeling left for him. The only thing that stopped me attempting to kill my husband was the thought of the stigma that my child would have to carry for life.

I have paid the deposit on our home and it is in our joint name. Also the contents are mine which I have bought.

My mother died recently and left me some money and I want to find a modest place for myself and son but I must do all this without my husband's knowledge so he will never be able to find me. Please help me.

Bedfordshire

Dear Mrs Pizzey,

The article in today's *News of the World* tightened the muscles of my throat as I had similar experiences more than fifty years ago. One hid such a thing then, to appear respectable. We farmed in Wales and with a bad sale it was a case of 'Look out!' I put the children to bed early so that they would not know.

Thank God wives today are not so soft. We farmed in England. I had the same treatment. I wrote to the doctor who came to see me on the market day when he wasn't there. He told me he could report him and advised me to leave him in a room by himself when in such a mood as he could not guarantee he would not hurt me. What did I get for safeguarding my family of four from such disgraceful conduct?

After my last son married I left him and for services rendered he left me nothing, but the grandchildren received £500 each, put in a building society many years ago in their name. I never had a penny of maintenance and had to work for myself. My sons have good jobs and I get the occasional cheque. I had £100, as that was all that was left after burial. No woman should hide under a cloak of respectability. Show the devils up. I wish I had.

Now you can see how my heartfelt sympathy goes to those wives. I was hit and yelled at if I was not interested in sex. How could anyone respond? Good luck to you and your helpers. At nearly eighty I'm no use to you.

Mrs B M

For all the efforts to keep the screaming soft, the neighbours know. They are usually embarrassed and will go to any lengths to pretend that they don't know. Remember Sue and Bert: only when Bert was breaking down the wall and coming into the next house did those neighbours call for the police.

One woman had taken in her neighbour the night her husband had shut her out after knocking her about, but when asked to act as a witness to support her neighbour's application for a separation order, she said she could not come forward *as her husband did not want her to get involved*.

When people can no longer ignore the fact that women are persistently maltreated in their homes, they make up a way of accounting for the suffering. It is then easier for them to carry on doing nothing about it. They need feel no guilt. So they believe, as if it were true, that the women are violent, or that they are women who like violent men. They can then say that the women deserve the treatment they get, i.e. that they must have done something to provoke it; or that they enjoy the treatment they get. Their suffering can then be dismissed as punishments justly deserved or wounds happily received. They can disregard the broken noses, the scarred lips and the ribs kicked in and the miscarriages ... With this account of oppression goes the point of view that people who stay in such terrible situations are spineless not to escape.

Every time we go to speak to meetings there is always someone who puts forward this argument. It is typical of the well-meaning public. Take as an example this letter:

To Jimmy Young,
BBC Radio 2.
Dear Jim,
I did not hear the interview with the two ladies regarding wife-beating yesterday so may have missed some relevant points. I would just like to ask: 'Why do these women put up with such appalling treatment?' Have they no self-respect? I realize that there may be cases when it would be difficult for a woman to leave her husband, especially when there are children, but I seem to recall reading or hearing about some who are quite well placed financially, without family commitments, and who *still* remain with their husbands. Personally it is the one thing I just would not tolerate. I always said a man would only hit me once and I've been married over forty years and had many ups and downs.
When I hear, as I have done, that wives have submitted to this

brutality for many years I cannot help wondering whether some of them don't in some perverse way get a kick out of being ill-treated. Please don't get me wrong, I have every sympathy with anyone who is badly treated, but I really do wonder sometimes what the real truth is when normal (?) grown-up people give and take such abnormal liberties. Please carry on with your interest in this and other human problems. I really do want to understand what impels people to behave as they do.

Whatever human beings do to one another, they never 'deserve' having their ribs kicked in or their noses broken. The few women who are violent themselves are the exceptions. Most women are innocent of any provocation. They will receive a broken nose for forgetting to iron some shirts, scalding water poured on them for providing a dinner their husband doesn't fancy. They just get hit.

Swanage, Dorset

Dear Madam,

Several weeks ago I watched your programme regarding battered wives and was shocked to see that so many women are beaten by their husbands.

My husband also beats me around terribly, whether he's drunk or not. He earns £36 a week and of this gives me £6 for housekeeping. This has to cover the milk, newspapers, hot dinners every night, food for the children and the dog.

I am twenty-two years old but am already a physical wreck. I'm 5'10" and weigh 8 st. 2, two stones lighter than when I first met him. I have had no new clothes for two years and he hits me if he thinks I look scruffy. He spends the rest of the money on drinks and clothes for himself. Our son lives in his cousin's cast-offs. I seem to spend most of my time in tears.

I used to be a happy girl, I have eight 'O' levels and two 'A' levels. I met my husband when I was training for higher management level in a hotel. He was in the public bar where I worked every night and also at lunchtimes and week-ends. It was because he was out every night that I took him to be single and so I started going out with him. It wasn't until a long time after this I found out he was married but then we were very much in love and unfortunately I was pregnant. He left his wife for me and their divorce is now nearly final. I still feel it was my fault for breaking up a marriage, although it was him who deceived me.

My husband took me everywhere with him until our son was born.

34

Since then he still goes out every night. On ten occasions he hasn't bothered to come home all night. He rolls in sometimes the next afternoon after the pubs have shut at lunch, expecting his meal to be on the table. If I ask him where he's been he just hits me.

I haven't been out for over four months. Because he only gives me £6 I have started a full-time job leaving my son with a baby-minder, something I don't like doing, but I go and see him every lunch-time. I used to keep my wages in the house but he found it and started helping himself for drinking money, so now I put it in the Post Office on pay day.

The strange thing is he loves his son and would never hurt him although he hits me in front of him. Just after Christmas he hit me and split my head open so I had to have four stitches, all because I complained that he spent all Christmas getting drunk in the pub, and yet he never bought our son a present.

A month ago he threw scalding water over me, leaving a scar on my right arm, all because I gave him a pie with potatoes and vegetables for his dinner, instead of fresh meat. When I tried to go to the doctor's surgery for treatment, he hit me until I couldn't go.

Two weeks ago he hit me full in the face because I went to my home town for the day. My lip was badly cut and the whole of my right side was so badly distorted that I couldn't face anybody for a week. As a result my top teeth seem dead and my cheekbone is broken.

My parents have completely disowned me and will not allow any communication to take place between myself and my two younger sisters. I have not seen or heard from them for months and with each day the longing to see them is greater.

All my friends in B — treated me as their long-lost sister when I visited them. Many times I have thought of committing suicide but every time it is the thought of my son that stops me. One of these days I may just go through with it.

Neither the local social worker nor council will help me.

I long to return to B — and start a new life among people who know and like me. I wrote to the B — council but they could not provide me with accommodation. I know that unless I return soon I shall commit suicide, I am so low. I don't love him any more but it seems that society is forcing me to stay with him.

He won't leave me as I do all his washing and cooking for him. I have to or he hits me. I am not writing this because I want somebody to feel sorry for me. It has just helped setting it down on paper. I just wish that society was made more aware of the fact that there are a lot of husbands like mine. Many people think that the wife must be to blame as well.

Here is an account by a twelve-year-old of why he came to Women's Aid:

I came to this house because my mother was battered by my Dad for no reason at all. One evening when I was coming from school my Mum and Dad quarrelled, then they started to fight and my Dad throwed my Mum to the other side of the room, then he throw cold water over her. He used to go out and stay for the weekend with his girlfriends and sometimes he hit us for no reason too. My Mum had left him before and he found out where we were staying and he said he would hit her again so we went back to him. It was all right for some weeks, then he start again, he start because he said that my Mum had a boyfriend. Every night my Dad would come and he would pick on her. I could never get no sleep. When my mother went shopping with my sister Sharon, they went to my Mum's friend for a while then went shopping. When she got home he said, 'Where have you been so long?' She told him, but he never believed her so he start to hit her. My Mum called Sharon to tell him but he still didn't believe her so my Mum told me to go and call her friend and tell my Dad where she was, so I ran over to her flat and she came. When she got inside she told him, then he kicked my Mum's friend out of the flat. She said she was going to call the police, but they never came.

My Dad asked us, 'Where is Tony?' but we said we didn't know. I ran to tell Tony not to go inside because Dad is going to hit you, so Tony was very scared and nervous. It was getting late and my mother told me to go out and to tell him to come in now because Dad had gone out. I found Tony and we both went home together. My Dad is the biggest bully around the flats. He punched her in the eye and on the arm and made bruises. My Mum had to go to the hospital with a white scarf round her eye. I had to follow and everyone was looking at her eye. When we reached there, they asked what had happened and she told them and they took X-rays on her eye. They put some stuff on them and we went home.

It was Sunday afternoon when I was playing football when my Dad came in. He asked, 'Where is your Mum?' I said at Mrs T, her friend's house. He went over there and knocked at the door. Someone opened it and he went straight in and punched my Mum in the face and walked straight out. My Mum's face started to bleed and her mouth was burst open. My Mum went home and my Dad said nothing.

In the morning he threatened her with a knife. He walked straight out. He came back and went straight in the bedroom. Five minutes later he came out and said, 'Where is my letter that was in my pocket?' He grabbed her and said, 'Find it.' And she told him that she never went in his pocket. He looked in the other side and there was his letter. Then he started to quarrel with her. He walked into the kitchen and got a long fork and hit her with it and he walked out and said he was not coming in tonight, and when he went my Mother said that she had got to leave this place, so she packed some things and we left the next morning to the Town Hall.

This is something that happened to my mother. When it was Christmas he buys us nothing nor on our birthday. Now you know why we are here.

As for the reaction, 'A lot of them like it', I've never met anyone who experiences this sort of violence – a broken jaw or a fractured spine – and wants to stay with it. No one wants to pay that price for a martyr's role. Most often it is a case of like it or lump it. That's the Catch-22: if the women put up with violence it's assumed they like it. In reality they stay and put up with it because they have nowhere else to go. Because they stay and put up with it they are assumed to like it and so they are blocked from finding somewhere else to go. So they stay and put up with it and it's assumed they like it. Many thousands of women are enclosed inside this vicious circle.

The psychiatrists' form of the 'they enjoy it' argument is that battered women are the sort of women who go out and sub-consciously choose men who will batter them. They consider the women 'victims' who can only be happy with a 'victimizer'. I will dispute with anyone the notion that women who marry men like these are natural victims. They aren't. They are just ordinary people with nowhere to go and no one to turn to. Just because a woman is in a 'victim' situation, that doesn't mean that she should be labelled a 'victim' and so given a life sentence.

Of course, if a psychiatrist *wants* to see battered women as natural victims, that's the way they'll appear to him. One psychiatrist who visited the house would not give up this point of view. He stuck to it despite all that we said to him. In the end the argument was not resolved but he went out into the garden. Janet and Jenny were so angry at him they booted him up the arse with a football. Even then he didn't react – he didn't smile or snarl or swear or shout or kick it back – he kept his cool and his opinions to the end of his visit and, sadly, took them away with him unchanged.

You see, society doesn't recognize that you can unknowingly marry a violent man. Your marriage can be declared null and void if you find that your spouse had a contagious venereal disease at the time of the marriage. You are not protected by the law if you find out, as Margaret did, that your spouse has a criminal record. It was much too late before Margaret found out about her husband. Her collar-bone had already been broken twice, and she was pregnant.

Nor do romantic young girls think to ask their fiancés, 'Have you ever had any mental treatment?' They rarely go for a psychiatrist's check-up before marrying, as many go to the doctor's. Many girls marry young without realizing what they are letting themselves in for.

Lucy was only about twenty-four when she came to the house. She had long blonde hair and a very gentle, mobile face with a smile that made everybody like her. She had two children. The eldest was seven, a very bright child with an enquiring mind. The first thing you noticed about him was his fierce and protective love for his sister, who was four. The children were indivisible. You could never get one to go anywhere without the other, and they would fight fiercely on each other's behalf.

Lucy had Julian when she was very young and she managed to keep him by working full-time with help from her mother who took care of the child during the day time.

Lucy's home life had been far from happy because Lucy's father had left home when she was very young and her step-father had been cruel and unkind to her. Having a baby gave her a loving unit of her own and she adored Julian, who was very much like her. She met her husband at a party, and during the time he was courting her he was kind and gentle. He was a very capable and intelligent man, which pleased Lucy because she should have continued her education. At the time she came to us she had just had two poems published.

Two days after she married him, he lost his temper over some shirts she'd forgotten to iron and he beat her up. She had black eyes and a broken nose. He didn't seem very remorseful and only then her mother-in-law volunteered the information that she had been advised to take him to a psychiatrist when he was seven because of his disturbed behaviour, but she hadn't got round to it. Lucy told me that one of his recurring nightmares was about a horse impaling itself. His mother told her that around seven years old he and a friend had shot staples at a horse which bolted and did indeed impale itself on some railings. He was always in trouble with the police. It turned out that he had several convictions for grievous bodily harm.

Things went from bad to worse, and then Sheila was born. The baby was only tiny when he tied Lucy up with wire and beat her in front of Julian, who was holding Sheila in his arms. Julian developed such a protective instinct that whenever there was violence he would get the baby out of her cot and hold her in his arms until the beating stopped. Sometimes the beating didn't stop at Lucy, and Julian too was beaten. She once had him admitted into hospital with his buttocks flailed raw by a caning. The hospital made no effort to report the matter to their medical social workers or to the N S P C C.

Lucy did go to social workers for help and they put her into temporary welfare accommodation, but when the social workers went home there was no one to protect her. Her husband often got into the huge unlit block of flats, broke into her room and threatened her. She explained that it was better to be at home where she knew where he was than sitting night after night not knowing if the footstep passing her door was him, or the car idling on the street was him waiting to catch her.

Very few people understand this kind of fear. It is the fear of knowing that someone is searching for you and will beat you when he finds you. In the mind of someone who has been badly beaten, this fear blots out all reason. The man seems to be omnipotent. I know the fear of streets that could possibly contain my enemy. Even now a particular cough or gesture can freeze me. So many times well-meaning social workers have said, 'I found her a nice flat and the next day she was back with him.' I don't think it takes much imagination to understand what goes on in the mind of someone who has been badly beaten.

Fortunately Lucy heard of us, and telephoned. She arrived and settled in on the office floor. Julian went to the school next door. Sheila was lovable and difficult and she fitted into the chaotic life around her with very little trouble.

Lucy said that as long as she didn't see her husband she would be able to make a break. She was like many women who come to the centre. She loved her husband but hated the beatings. If we could remove the beatings she would go back like a shot. I didn't think there was much hope where her husband was concerned and I privately hoped she would never go back. We applied for a divorce for cruelty and we waited for her legal aid certificate.

Lucy began to work full-time, sorting out other people's problems. She had the warmth and compassion needed to get other women to feel at home when they came in. As the weeks went by she talked less of her husband, but we all knew that she felt very responsible for him for she'd said he had no one but her. Like a lot of men who are mentally disturbed and violent, he had no friends.

On the day of the court case, the solicitor forgot to take her address off the papers that were served on her husband, so he found her and he telephoned, broken-hearted. He begged and pleaded, and she forgot the times she had been to hospital with broken ribs and a fractured jaw, the time they patched up her nose only to find that they had to do it again because he'd smashed it before it had time to set, the time he had stood with a knife at Julian's throat daring her to let the social worker in, and all the times she had been so bruised in the mornings that Sheila had put her arms about her, crying, 'Daddy do that – bad Daddy,' and run to her father and tried to hammer him with her little fists.

Lucy left one morning after writing me this letter.

Dear Erin,

I am going back. I promise at the first sign of violence I'll be back. I am an emotional coward, I cannot allow myself to reason that it will fail. I need to be loved for some unknown reason by him alone.

I think in a way I will not allow myself to admit defeat. I cannot let go. I love him, a part of me tells me it's wrong, especially for the kids.

Underneath him somewhere deep, too deep to have shown itself a lot up till now, is a sensitive, sentimental lamb.

I can understand how Caroline felt, as this in a way is how I feel. Also the inability to concede to defeat.

I have talked to the kids about this and I feel that they understand. Sheila asked me a couple of weeks ago, in fact the day I first went to court, when we would go back. She said that Daddy needs help but will not let us give it to him. She reasoned that if we did try, maybe he would accept our help. At the time I could not give her an answer.

I know how she feels as I felt the same about my stepfather. I know you are going to say that in the end I hated him, too true, there is no denying this fact. I am hoping to prevent this.

I was away on holiday when the news came through that she was dead. She had rammed her Mini into a tree on an empty road. Julian had run away from a row. No one really knows much about what happened but she had said that she couldn't allow herself to reason that she would fail. I knew she couldn't win.

Her husband buried her in a coffin lined with pink velvet. Several women from the centre were there. He now has both the children. Julian's school are worried about him – he keeps arriving covered in bruises – and they got in touch with his grandmother. She told us and we alerted the N S P C C and the social services, but Julian's father refused to let the social worker in, so nothing has yet been done to help them.

As long as the myths of beauty and the beast, the princess and the frog hold strong, young girls will believe that the love of a good woman can save any man, that the ugly frog will turn into a prince once the princess takes him into her bed and kisses him.

Anyone who has been badly knocked about loses all sense of reality and ability to cope. Battered women are almost permanently in a shocked state. The constant fear of another beating leaves them very tense and nervous. Some can't eat, others sleep little. Even the toughest find it hard to fight off the depression which has overwhelmed the writer of this letter:

Croydon

Dear Madam,
I have this minute heard your broadcast on the B B C radio programme *You and Yours*. I am forty-three years of age, my husband is forty-four, our son is four years. I have been hit many times by him, as well as being punched on the side of my head by his sister (whose house we rent). When my son and I came home from hospital after

his birth I was holding my baby at the time. This awful business still has the power to make me feel sick even now. My husband ordered us out. I left with our boy and obtained a living-in job with the help of the local Moral Welfare Association. My husband arrived and made such a scene that I had to come back. Again the same thing happened, again the social services acquired for me a living-in post which floundered, too many people were suffering.

On receiving a promise by him to buy our own house which we viewed in Oxford, I agreed to return here until such time as we arranged a mortgage. This arrived; my husband then wrote to his solicitor cancelling the house purchase. This was two months ago.

Since then I have been punched again and, more important, my son was struck on his thigh by my husband, using his leather belt. I intervened, snatched it off him and struck him. He took it from me easily – he is 6′ 2″ and strong, we stand no chance, my boy and me. I am permanently on watch. I visited the doctor, who brought in the health visitor. Once I started to tell them, I cried and couldn't stop crying. The doctor gave me a prescription for tranquillizers which stop the tears but also deactivate me. I sit and sit and when the tablets wear off the tears come back. I am this moment waiting for the promised visit from the social worker. No definite date or time was given.

Today I heard what you said on the radio. At least I haven't suffered permanent physical damage as has the lady who was interviewed, but I do know the possibility and probability is there. I don't go to church but I have taken to praying.

On the positive side, I have started divorce proceedings. Legal aid has yet to be granted. Miss E, the health visitor, seems to appreciate the seriousness of the situation. My family are fed up with my marital problems (who can blame them?) but they don't see my husband here. They have seen him crying and saying, ‘I want my wife and son.’ Also, the power of action has gone from me, lethargy, depression, etc. I do not present an attractive picture. The last I saw of my sister with whom I stayed for a week, some weeks ago, was when my husband turned up, stayed, and the atmosphere became strained, affecting her schoolboy sons. She asked him to take me and my son ‘home’. I had previously asked for a loan from another sister who had agreed in order that I could pay a month's rent, but have heard nothing. I have exactly £6 cash and £10 premium bonds. My husband, who previously wanted ‘you and the filthy brat out’, now makes a big fuss of wanting the boy. Life without him is no life for me. I am now in a state called agoraphobia. My little one knows, without knowing why his Mummy is unhappy. He is aggressive at times. His need is other children. We see no one. Please write to us.

42

Years and years of cruelty and vicious persecution can knock the determination out of anybody. One woman who wrote to us had endured a nightmare marriage for thirty years. Time and again she'd tried to break out. She often went to her mother's, but her husband had broken in there and taken her back. The police never did anything to stop him because it was a marital quarrel. Nobody else wanted to be involved. After all, she did have a roof over her head, didn't she? He always kept her short of money. She took a job once, but she had to work twelve hours to earn overtime to make her salary equal to a man's and that meant leaving the children alone in the evenings. After six months of that she gave it up. Each time she and her children went back to her husband, he got her pregnant again. Each time they were treated worse, because he knew they could not choose but take it. He used to taunt her with, 'Where can you go? What can you do?'

This woman was caught in a trap. There was no way out but suicide, and she once tried that. Her trap – which her husband made for her – was her seven children. They were the ones who suffered, through no fault of their own. Her only mistake was marrying the man in the first place. Is this spinelessness? She knew well she wanted to get out, and tried often, but she was trapped inside the family.

All these arguments – that women provoke, deserve or enjoy being beaten – are useless because they don't account for the facts.

As soon as the word got round that there was somewhere that women who suffer violence could take refuge, women were coming and they have never stopped coming. By May 1973, we were taking nearly 100 telephone calls a day. The little house was getting so full that we had to put mattresses down in the hall for people to sleep on. The usual number of residents was about thirty women and children.

By this time we were competing with the rats at the house. Obviously with only one lavatory and no bathroom, hygiene was almost impossible. Most mothers could cope but some that had been particularly badly treated were almost incapable of cleaning up after themselves. With many small babies it was a major battle to keep the nappies from piling up in corners and the dirty washing from asphyxiating the inmates.

We had been looking for another house, as the demolition of Belmont Terrace was imminent, but all through the first part of 1973 we'd had no success. Then in the early summer we received a letter from a man called Neville Vincent. He said he had some experience of property and would we contact him if we would like some help. I was pretty cynical about this sort of offer by this time, but sent one of the girls to see him and she reported back that he seemed OK. So three of us went to his office, which turned out to be a very imposing place in Sloane Square.

He was a very rare sort of man in that he didn't bullshit, he merely listened to our account of life at 2, Belmont Terrace and said he would visit us. He did within a few days and then he sat on the mattress in the office talking to everyone in the house – people liked him.

He called us back and said he thought we must have a bigger house so he advised us to go and look for one and he would put the matter to the board of directors of Bovis. To their everlasting credit they agreed.

We scoured Chiswick looking at large dilapidated houses and then one morning we were given the details of 369, Chiswick High Road. From the moment we walked into the hall we knew it was just right for a community house. It had huge rooms and a large garden but, best of all, it had a big basement area which could be converted to a playgroup space and playrooms for the older children.

The place was totally derelict but to us it was luxury. We had three inside toilets, and after thirty-five women and children to one outside WC it was heaven. There was no hot water but at least there was space and the children went wild in the garden.

Number 369 filled up as soon as we opened the door there. We were only licensed for thirty-six people at Number 369 but there are often 130 women and children in the house. Hounslow Council are sympathetic and acknowledge that we are doing our best, given the unique situation. But having us on their patch is enough to give any councillor heart-failure, for if our organization were to collapse, Hounslow could well find themselves responsible for two hundred women and children. Of course one day we can have five mothers and their fifteen children sleeping in rows on the floor and the next day two huge families may decide to return to the matrimonial home either through the courts or to try a reconciliation, so the numbers sometimes keep steady.

I suppose it would have been much easier to have an admissions policy which said once we were full, no more. But, as all the mothers say, 'I can't turn away a sobbing mother – supposing that had been me?' At first the children were sleeping four to a mattress. The mothers lay on the floor, and the ones who were pregnant we found beds for.

It's a sobering thought: those women who came to sleep on the floor with their children must have left unimaginable suffering to be able to bear this way of life. There's no privacy in the house and no chance of peace and quiet. There's always someone waiting to have a wash and often no hotplates free on the three cookers in the one communal kitchen. In the school holidays the children are all over the place: eighty children in a 100 ft garden.

In spite of the appallingly crowded conditions, there is a marvellous atmosphere in the house. It works because women who have been living with violence are shut off from other people, and so are their children; Women's Aid forces them out of their isolation. When they come into the house they are crowded together with many others who've been through the same kind of suffering. They have to communicate. Often for the first time since they married they are talking to someone who understands what it's like, because she's been through the same herself. They can also listen and recognize what others have been through. They can see they aren't alone.

We've opened more houses. One is outside London. It's for the women who have been seriously harassed by their husbands. That's full. Another is on short loan from the Notting Hill Housing Trust – that's full with one family per room. To date we've only received one of the five houses so magnificently promised in March 1974 by Paddy O'Connor of the GLC, but that's full too. We will easily fill the other four when they are made available. We've more houses outside London promised and many families waiting to move into them and we are still being swamped with requests for help.

Other women's aid groups through Britain have had the same experience. When space is made available it is immediately taken up by people who badly need it. Some have been needing refuge for years. In Glasgow they have been putting up thirty-one children and fifteen women in a four-room flat. They are worried about the overcrowding rules and about the danger if there was a fire (the flat's above ground level) and they've had to turn women away. In Brixton the house was full within days of opening.

Wife-beating has gone on for hundreds of years. Up to about 150 years ago it was recognized in British law that a man had a right to chastize and confine his wife. He can still rape his wife without breaking the law. For ages wife-beating was thought to be a working-class activity, for the middle- and upper-class women never let on.

As far as I can see the reason why 'battered wives' are getting a hearing is that for the first time a middle-class woman has said, 'It's happened to me'. That makes it respectable and all the more shocking. Now – just as 'battered babies' were once called 'manslaughter' – wife-beating has become the 'battered-wife syndrome'. But it's not enough to call it a new name and then carry on as before.

Chapter 3

Battered Mothers, Beaten Children

THE following letters are typical of the ones we are receiving every day at Women's Aid. Some women are through their suffering and on the other side and write to give us support and confirm their experience. Others are asking for help from us:

Coventry

Dear Madam,

I missed the phone number when it must have been shown but was dying to phone you but could not get the telephone number.

I have been through all the ordeals that your women have said on this programme.

Fifteen years ago I was at last free from the cruelty when he was asked to go for a period while court proceedings progressed. I was not believed. When proof was desired it was changed round that I was at fault and asked for it. It was changed round that I was mentally ill as such that if I screamed, he said, I screamed so he hit me to stop me but this was not so. I screamed because he hit me.

Yes, it is true that you get twice as much back when you try to defend yourself.

I have brought up a son and a daughter but courts and people seem to believe him instead of me. I think this is because he had a good job and is now a works manager and was a freeman of the city.

I do not get any money now and haven't had since my two left school, one to college, although he was supposed to pay me two pounds. I would lose again if I go to court as I have so many times, as the courts seem to have been on his side.

The courts allowed him to sell our house, jointly owned. I refused to sell so it had to be a court hearing but I had by that time had my children seven years on my own and he gave me £4, and paid the mortgage and bills. My son was about to sit his 'A' levels but the court still turned us out and told me to go to the council. I had worked for a deposit for the house. He joined a self-build scheme. He got to the stage he wanted nothing to do with taking us out or paying and demanded sex and beat me terribly. Sometimes I got frightened and ran out in my nightdress. He would lock the door and I had to sleep in the garage, frozen.

Still, good luck to your work and I hope you relieve a lot of women from this torment, which is dreadful. I tried everything but failed to get help.

Sincerely,

Andover

Dear Mrs Pizzey,

Please could you advise me what to do. I have had eight children and I am nearly forty-seven years old. I have still three children at home, the youngest is seven years old. My husband keeps saying I'm mad and keeps on hitting me and whipping me. I've had a broom over my head and needed medical treatment, a dislocated shoulder, bruises all over me and two black eyes and kicked in the ribs. I've been to the police and they don't know what to do about domestic quarrels. I've been to the Samaritans and to the solicitor. The solicitor told me, I can't do a lot about a separation or divorce as you are living under the same roof. He had been to see my doctor with me to try and get me in a mental home. My doctor has given me nerve pills last week because my nerves are beginning to go and he told my husband I am not mad.

My children scream because he shouts and hits me in front of them. He has thrown me out at night and told me to go but I can't leave the children and it is a job to get a room with children. He said if I went he would get the children in a home. He has never bought them any clothes and I have to keep on to him to buy the children a pair of shoes twice a year and I can't afford to buy clothes for them. You can see what I'm up against.

Don't you think the law is wrong and there should be a law for husbands like mine? Please send a reply to – as I don't want him to know, as I would get it worse.

Some mothers and children have been so badly treated that it may take them years to get back on their feet. One of our bitterest sorrows is that we don't yet have the money to provide enough support and peace and quiet for the women who are so broken down they are like zombies and for their children who are so disturbed. The confusion of this letter tells its own story:

Brighton

Dear Madam,

Hearing you speak made me feel you are ashamed, as I know I am,

48

of admitting you are subject to being beaten by your husband and find it hard to talk about.

Later in the week Erin, speaking to Jimmy on the telephone, of course pinpointed why you are afraid of rushing for help and so putting up with it: because of a reprisal.

My husband does not drink but is an epileptic and when I married him he had frequent attacks. Now it is kept completely under control on stronger drugs.

It is a fact, medical knowledge has found that most epileptics are violent. When I was single I was a State Enrolled Nurse and on many occasions finished our friendship. This wasn't because of his complaint; I didn't think we were suited.

He is one of six children but, being the youngest, was spoilt and never learned to give and take, and the home was isolated from the village by a mile and I believe out of school he didn't communicate with children his age.

He became very selfish and demanding. His family were always pushing us together, especially mother and two of his sisters, invitations to stay, to visit and parties.

When we had parted the family finally realized. The older sister came to see me as if they had no idea and [were] just showing kindness.

On my twenty-first birthday was the time I found it hard to refuse this friendship for good. Then my husband was at college and so he didn't earn money himself and he came to the nurses' home I was living in, after being parted for a month. I refused to go to the door, the domestic made an excuse up and we discussed how to get round not seeing him. He knew I was in and just coming off night duty.

He came back with a pile of presents: a watch from him, leather writing-case from his parents, jewellery, etc. I was told you most certainly must see him as they will not do for anyone else and shops wouldn't take them back and it would hurt everyone to refuse them, so I finished up marrying. Somehow I knew I didn't want to.

This was pure selfishness from his family, they needed someone who would be able to take care of him and he was soon to be going away from home to work.

He is a chartered engineer and because I've been loyal and have not witnesses alive to prove his cruelty my divorce is still going on from March 1972, when the last violent incident took place. The only person to hear him hitting me was our landlady –. She died several months later; the worry had made her ill, knowing she had a violent man in the house. She was a widow and was becoming very neurotic.

The last attack on 31 March last year was because I said the wallpaper my youngest son, then seven years old, had chosen didn't seem suitable for his bedroom; all the same pattern in two different colours – too dazzling. I was standing at the kitchen sink when suddenly the lounge door opened and he threw two rolls of wallpaper at me with great force, hitting me on my waist, and I found myself crumpled up on the floor in great pain and couldn't call for my daughter to help. All I was capable of doing was moaning.

My daughter who was eleven years came down and wanted to know what I was doing on the floor, and was eventually able to get me up. She was afraid to stay in the house and went out the back door. Some twenty minutes later one more roll of paper was thrown and missed, but damaged the oven.

Had I had my back to him when he threw the first two rolls I believe my spine would have been broken – the force of the first two rolls were thrown at great strength. He came into the hall an hour later to hit me, and my daughter saw this and screamed. This stopped him. Her younger brother came running to see what was wrong. They were both clinging to each other, crying.

I was unable to get them in for dinner. I phoned the police. He [the policeman] arrived, brought the children in and spoke to my husband. My husband shouted and argued and the policeman came back and said, 'For goodness sake, go and see a solicitor.'

Later in the evening my husband asked me to say *I* was sorry. I ignored what he said, so he came across and pulled my arm off the chair, pushed me on to the settee and struck me several times. He was holding me tightly down and when he moved slightly I was able to struggle free. I left the house to phone a doctor.

Later the police rang for the doctor. He came in the early afternoon. My doctor talked to me for some time and wasn't willing to go into the house until my husband had time to calm down, but suggested we went to the police and get advice from them. On the way a police car passed us in the opposite direction, so my doctor turned round and caught him up.

The doctor opened up his surgery to have discussion and it was agreed we must not be left under the same roof for the night. I was willing to take a taxi to London, along with my daughter who I couldn't leave behind. My doctor came home with me and by this time my husband was in bed and when he got up and heard the idea put to him he insisted he would be the one to go to get a hotel for the night.

The police were waiting in a car outside. I insisted they did not come, as this caused arguments. When the doctor left, my husband was dressing and my doctor said he would ring in about twenty minutes to make sure I was alone. My husband was present when this was said. My husband left about 1 a.m. and five or six times during the night the phone rang constantly till it was answered and the caller immediately put the phone down.

My husband returned at 6 a.m. He was away for five hours only but he was unable to get in as I had bolted the doors, knowing nothing of the mood he'd be in. Rang the police briefly stating what had happened. Opening the door to him he greeted my trembling daughter with smiles and went to the kitchen to make a hot drink. I kept an eye open to catch the police before they knocked. Was speaking to them and our dog started barking. My husband went to the door and went to the police and spoke to them himself. The police sergeant made some sarcastic remark to me about not being a taxi service, only to come to homes where it was absolutely necessary. I had this thrown back at me dozens of times.

My beatings have not been frequent but usually over money. Once in a fury he knocked over an oil stove and was in hospital for three months with burns. His wages ceased after a while and I had to live on National Assistance. He gives me £3 a week, which is an impossible amount.

As soon as he knew I was getting a divorce he started to buy my son clothes, a thing he has never done before, and then started to buy things for all the children, but the bitter atmosphere in this house upsets everyone.

My parents are dead so I have no one to help.

Some are lucky and find help from friends or relatives:

After listening to the lady who spoke about wife-beatings on your programme I had to put pen to paper and try to give others hope.

I was married at seventeen and, I am sorry to say, to a sadist, very charming to everyone but his family.

After the first week of marriage the beatings started and continued for three terrifying years. I suffered malnutrition, broken bones and various other things including knife wounds and mental stress.

If, as I was, some women are too frightened to even attempt to leave, it is even harder. I was lucky. A friend helped me to leave and lent me the money to go nearly 200 miles away with my small daughter. She was then two years old and is now a happy ten-year-old. I have re-married and her stepfather is very loving towards her.

My husband now has nursed me through four nervous breakdowns and made life bearable again. You can never forget the past but if like me you are lucky to find someone who understands the situation that you have been through, with love and kindness can bring you back the happiness that years of beatings and mental suffering have destroyed.

The only thing I still cannot do, even after all this time, is to go out alone. If not pressed I would not even go shopping.

I still live with the fear of my first husband but slowly that is also fading into the background.

One of the most horrifying aspects of violence is seeing the children coming in with bruised faces and terrible welts from beating. Fatima's two boys – aged two and a half and one – had huge bruises over their backs. Their father used to punch them and keep on punching until they were insensible. Those boys cried all day and night. We had them checked by doctors and they said there was nothing wrong with them – they were just terrified of everything and everybody because all their experience consisted of blows and curses, as you will see from Fatima's account.

I came to England in 1964 to have an operation on my eye and I met my husband because our parents knew each other, and when I was in hospital he and his elder brother came to visit me. They said, 'When you are better you can come and stay with us.' Soon after I came out of hospital he asked me to marry him, but I said 'No', as I had a good job at home.

The day before I was due to leave he decorated his room and said we would get married. They locked me in that room and he raped me. I was then ashamed as I am a Moslem and come from a very strict home. I could not then marry anybody else.

I went back to my own country but I did not tell anybody what had happened. I was a respectable girl and my parents would have been ashamed of me. He kept writing to me that he loved me and to come back. He said nobody would marry me now that I was not a virgin and that I only had one eye, so I should be pleased to marry him. I came back in December 1965 and we were married in a Moslem mosque. He drank quite a lot. Every day he would drink but he would never beat me, but I think it was because we were living with an elderly English couple and he was afraid to hit me then as he respected them. When the English woman died, her husband went to live with his daughter, and it was when we were on our own that he started beating me. He would kick me with his foot and punch me. Once he beat me in my eyes and I thought I would be blind.

In my third pregnancy I had an asthma attack and he put a pillow over my head and a girl from upstairs saw it and rang for an ambulance. I was in hospital for a few days but I didn't tell anybody what happened. The girl told the doctor and the police that he had beaten me and they said they would take action against him, but I said to say nothing as I had two other children at home and it would be terrible when I went back.

Once he tried to strangle me at night and I was crying and somebody passed by and knocked on the door. He didn't open the door and by the time the police came he had kicked me down the stairs and pushed me out of the door. The policemen came and picked me up and when they asked my husband what he thought he was doing, he said to me, 'Hello darling, come in.'

He does not work but for a long time drew sickness benefit until our doctor refused to give him any more certificates, and now he draws unemployment benefit. He only has a job for a few weeks and then gives it up or gets the sack.

Last Wednesday he was beating me again and again and he locked me in. On Thursday he was beating me again in the night time. I ran downstairs to get away from him and went into the kitchen and I closed the door but he just kicked the door open. I ran into the back garden and held the door shut with my hands. He shouted that he was going to kill me. I called the neighbour next door and she came over the fence and behind my back garden is a factory and some men opened the window and asked, 'What is the matter?' I shouted, 'My husband is going to kill me.' My neighbour went to the front door and my husband said, 'It is none of your business,' and the neighbour said she would get the police.

That night he went out and got drunk and he came back at 2 p.m. and started beating me. He had taken my son with him and my son said they had been to a pub and a betting shop. If I don't argue with him he does not hit me, but sometimes he just used to hit me to make me talk.

The next day at 5 a.m. he started banging my head. Then he kicked me. I closed my eyes and he just beat me in front of my children and he stamped on my feet. I was beaten all day and night. He did not go out all day. My nephew came but did not interfere because he was frightened. I was folding the bedspread and he got behind me and pulled my hair and kicked me. I could not do anything. He went upstairs to drink and I picked up the two youngest children and said to my nephew, 'Do not let him know that I am going out,' but as I said that he was looking down over the banisters, and as I was going out he pulled me in again. I ran out again but I only got a few yards and he caught me up. I saw two women talking and I grabbed their hands and asked for their help. He said, 'Come on, darling.' One woman called her son out and said she would send for the police but my husband and her son had an argument. I stayed with the ladies

53

for a while. I told the ladies he was beating me and the ladies talked to him and said to m 'Why don't you go home and talk about it and then it will be alright.' I went back to the house because I had asked her to phone the police and thought the police were coming. The lady thought it would be all right with my husband and did not phone the police. The third time I got in again and he pushed me and kicked me with his feet and said he would kill me with a karate chop so there would be no mark on my body to show how I died. He beat me and beat me and I felt myself getting weaker and weaker and thought I was going to die.

I felt so weak and didn't want to die in that house and my nephew was here. I told my nephew, 'Don't make any noise,' and just opened the door. I only took the baby and thought later I would get somebody to come back for the other two. I ran down the road and collided with a man and asked him to help me. He laughed and said, 'How can I help?' I explained and he took me into a pub which he was painting. The lady there phoned for the police and gave me water. When the police came and saw me they said they were going to take me to hospital but I said I had two other children in the house and they were not safe. They took me to the social worker and the woman there said, 'Your husband talks like a good man.'

I told the policeman to bring me home and get my babies. The policeman talked to my husband and he said, 'It is my wife and I can do what I like. I will even hit her now in front of you.'

I told the policeman to bring me to the social worker, Miss Williams, who is dealing with our case. Miss Williams said I could not stay in her office but agreed to come back to the house with me to collect my things.

I told Miss Williams I wanted a place where nobody would know where I was staying. Miss Williams said to me to see a solicitor and get a divorce. I said to her where shall I stay during this time and she said, 'In your home, of course.'

I do not possess a key to my house and my eldest child went into a neighbour's house and then opened the kitchen door. I went in with Miss Williams. My husband was on the bed and as I went into the bedroom to get my things he threw an ashtray at me and said, 'So you have come back have you?' and I said, 'I am going away for a few days,' and got the eldest boy to quickly pack some things. Miss Williams was downstairs and I got her to come up and she said to him, 'Your wife is only going away for a few days.' He looked at me and smiled and said in French, 'I will kill you wherever you are.' Miss Williams smiled and said, 'Don't stay longer than a few days.' Nobody thinks he is terrible because he is so polite to them and tells lies.

I have nobody to go to, all our friends know him so I cannot stay with them. His brother is not interested and would only take me back to him. I have written to my mother and told her for the first time what sort of life I have lived. He has often beaten the children, especially the younger two, throwing them against the wall.

Fatima's children improved rapidly. Before long the two little ones began to smile at us. The older boy went to school with the other children. Miss Williams only changed her tack when Fatima's husband threatened to throw acid in her face if she didn't tell him where his wife was. (Up to then she hadn't believed that he was violent because he was 'such a charming man'.) So the husband arrived at the door, begging and weeping for his wife to go back. She refused and said he was to go away and leave her alone. She did go back in the end, but it didn't work. He became more violent and she's now left him.

While Fatima's children were only beaten by their father, some women come into Women's Aid and we realize very soon that they batter their children. In some families the mother is battered and then turns on the children out of rage and despair. It's not difficult to see why this happens, for at one time or another, if a woman's honest, she will admit to herself, 'If it wasn't for the children . . .' She feels pity for her children but she sometimes also resents them.

Laura was only fourteen when she was raped by her father and gave birth to a deformed and subnormal child. In fact her father had molested her on and off for years and after this event he turned on the younger sisters in the family. In an effort to get away Laura married a man of nineteen. They set up home, but before long he started to knock her about. He had a good job and worked hard but as he couldn't read or write he was unable to accept promotion. He'd had an awful background. What probably turned him off human beings for life was the death of his sister, who was the only person he loved during his long trek from one children's home to another. She died because her husband threw an electric fire into her bath when she was seven months pregnant. This left Laura's husband horrified by pregnancy. When Laura found she was pregnant the serious beatings started and he repeatedly left home. The baby was born but the tensions remained, and when Laura came to me she told me she had had seven miscarriages and this one baby and she was desperate to get sterilized because she was always pregnant and she was always beaten.

The first time she telephoned me to say she had hit her baby and made his nose bleed, I called her social worker and said please go and see her immediately and, if it would help, bring her to Women's Aid and we would look after her and the child for a while. The social worker went down to see Laura and told her she would be prosecuted if she hit the child.

No hospital would agree to sterilize Laura – they said she was too young and might want more children. It was arranged after endless arguments and long talks, that her husband should have a vasectomy, but the waiting list was six months and that was too long. By that time Laura had a second child who lives almost permanently in hospital because she is always on the edge of battering. Her husband visits her from time to time and usually leaves her a black eye. Her little boy is probably deaf in both ears from battering and finally it has been agreed that she should be sterilized. Her own decision, made before the second baby was conceived, was the right one.

Sometimes, as in the case of Sarah, the husband made a favourite of her middle boy and when he had beaten her he would take the boy out and buy him a present, so that by the time the boy was seven or eight his mother's beatings came to mean rewards and he would hang around and watch, laughing, to endear himself to his Dad, but when his Dad went out then Sarah would lash out and beat him. That resolved itself when the boy stabbed his classmate with a pair of scissors and was put into a children's home. But nothing has been done to protect the two other children at home.

In Mary's case we realized that she was very retarded, which she covered up very well until you really started to get to know her. She could not read or write but she was very beautiful and had such a lovely childish way with her that it was hard not to love her.

She beat her two small children. Not in a cruel or sadistic way, but she reacted to them as though she were a child of the same age. I think her mental age was about ten. When we told her social worker about our fears, she agreed that they did know that she battered the children and they had tried to keep an eye on her. Well, we discovered that it took more an than eye to stop her lashing out at the children and soon a rota of mothers cared for the children and Mary lay in bed nursing another pregnancy. She was twenty-six, she told us. She had one miscarriage, two children died, one by smothering and one a cot death, and now these two little girls she had with us. We discovered that both the deaths had question marks over them.

What Mary needs is community care and probably for the rest of her life. She and her husband both signed sterilization forms, for she decided that this was to be her last pregnancy, but again the surgeon decided that she was too young. She went into hospital and we looked after her children and during that time tried everywhere for somewhere to put her. Mary was more than we could handle and we decided we should ask for help for her. With all the publicity about battered babies it should not have proved difficult. In fact we got precisely nowhere. All the social services could offer us was bed and breakfast if we didn't keep her. It would be a death warrant for her children, so we took her back. At the moment she has gone back to her husband, but it will end in tragic circumstances because, even though the health visitors visit every day, they are not there all night. If we get large community centres for mothers and children she will be first on the list.

Few women let their resentment against their children turn them to battering them unless they have themselves been repeatedly beaten in childhood. Jane was beaten in childhood and beaten in marriage, and she beats all her four children. Yet Sally, the eldest, sailed through to grammar school in spite of (or perhaps it was because of) the disruptions and distractions of having both her parents drunk and violent and her being the one who was virtually running the household.

Time and time again I've seen children whose mothers are violent towards them taken away and put into care. I've noticed that this is often disastrous for both mother and child. A beaten child can form a very strong attachment for his mother, despite the beatings. The woman needs a child, so if one is taken away she will go out and conceive another. Social security benefits are a pittance, so she may go from man to man for support. Meanwhile the State is spending about £30 a week on caring for each of her children. Give the mother £30 a week and she will have a chance to keep her family together. Taking a child into care doesn't resolve the mother's situation, it simply replaces one problem with another. I see a future where the social agencies will let mother and child stay together and take them both into care if it is needed.

Ros spent two months at the centre. She came to us after she'd run away from her husband. She'd met him in a mental hospital where she was receiving treatment after yet another breakdown. Ros was one of the legion of deprived women that come into the centre. Ian, she told us, was cruel and wicked (which he wasn't) and they all lived in one room, which was making things much worse. She had two children with her and it was obvious that the older one was very deeply disturbed. We contacted her social worker who told us that she had known Ros for years and felt that very little could be done for her. Ros's story seemed so complicated that I asked her to write it out for us. This is how it began:

I am writing this story because I feel it might help other people, single or married women. All my life I have been searching for the impossible: love and security. You see, when I was a child I never had anyone to love me. People turned their backs. When I was in my mother's womb I was so warm, I had nothing to worry about, but then came the day of my departure from this warm and very secure sanctuary – and my life began.

I stayed with my mother for a month in hospital, then I was taken to a house where no one cared what happened to me. I was put in dirty beds and given dirty bottles, and my arms were tied to the bed in case I fell off, so the people could go out. After a while my stomach got fed up with dirty bottles and I had to go to hospital because I had gastro-enteritis and also they thought that I would die – it would have solved a lot of people's problems if I had done: my mother would have been able to go back to her own children – but, alas, it did not work out that way. After the priest came and gave me the last rites I became better. I had been spared to carry on my life – but to what purpose? I did go back to this woman's home and stayed there until I was six. She had other children, a boy and a girl and anything that was brought for me by my mother (whom I used to address as Aunty) was taken away from me and given to them. I used to be shut out in a yard in the rain and thunderstorms. I used to be in a bed with only my vest in the cold weather.

Anyway, soon they had enough of me and had to think of somewhere else for me to go so I was sent to a convent in Chertsey. Then I was taken from there and sent to Willesden to another convent. Then I became ill and was sent to a convalescent home in Dover and after that I was sent to a place in Suffolk. As the war was on then and it was evacuation time for all children I expect there were many like me, frightened and scared and missing their mums and dads dreadfully. Soon I was brought back to my mother and father and started a new life in a French school. I did not take to it very well. I wish now I had. I was then put into another school where everyone used to laugh at me. I had to wear skirts down to my ankles, and they used to call me 'Drainpipe' and say, 'Watch yourself on the way home or you will fall down a drain.' I never had a friend, not my mother nor my father liked me.

I left school and went to work so my father could drink a little more. He used to have a pail in his room as we had to go down three flights for an outside toilet and when I went in one day he said I had not ironed his shirts properly and got a piece of cloth, put it in the urine bucket and pushed it in my mouth. I used to roll his cigarettes before I went to bed, polish his boots and was told to sit in the kitchen quiet – he used to go to bed at 7 o'clock at night.

My mother used to work all day. She did not sleep with him and she did not like him. He did not like me either. After a while he stopped talking to me and used to leave notes out of what I had to do. I very rarely saw my mother and I used to get so frightened sometimes when I was in bed as I used to feel his hands on me. My mother would come home at 1 a.m. with a man who was working at the pub where she was a cook.

A dreadful thing did happen to me one day when I was at school. I felt something on the chair and I thought I had had an accident. I looked to see what it was and saw it was blood. I ran out of the classroom and to where my mother worked and told her about it and she said, 'Don't be silly, you get these things. Now go back to school.' I still did not find out what it was. Anyway my mother and father thought it was disgusting to talk about such things, sex and menstruation, so I still believed when I went to work at a printer's that babies came from gooseberry bushes, and the girls used to tease me. I was doing a training course in the printer's but the laughing and teasing still went on. My skirts were silly and shoes and hair and I was too shy and withdrawn to make a friend, but I longed for one. I used to hear them talking about going out, to pictures, etc., but I was never invited. Anyway, I packed it up.

Then I went into Woolworths on the book counter and just across the road from us there used to be a bookshop and a boy used to come in fairly often and buy reading material, and I became quite friendly with him and I used to meet him, but my mother and father did not know. I used to say I had to work late and they took my word for it. For a while it became quite serious with this boy. I used to make all sorts of excuses to get out on Sunday, I would go to watch reserve teams play. I used to go to his mum and dad afterwards, and they were very nice people. I was so happy that someone cared. Then came the day when he went into the army and on his leave he would come and see me at Woolworths, and then he asked me to marry him. Well, I was happy and also very worried. I had to face my parents with this news. I told my mother, she told my father and he said, there and then, 'No'. He asked my mother to get my boyfriend's address which I had to give and he wrote a very nasty little letter to him and said he could not support me and forbade him to see me, but I still carried on seeing him and we used to go out with his friends and their girl-friends. One night when I went home my father got hold of me and told me to wipe the dirty muck off my face and wash it and I defied him for the first time ever and I had a jolly good hiding off him. He did not like me wearing lipstick or make-up. Then this boy I was courting went overseas to Singapore and said he would write to me very regularly and I had to catch the postman every morning because my mother would sometimes take my letters and open them and destroy them.

While my boyfriend was away I went on working and I asked the supervisor if I could work late, dressing counters, etc., because the thought of going home to a lonely place really did bother me. Anyway time passed and I got more fed up with my father's drinking and my mother working all night that one day I went into the chemist and bought some aspirins and calamine lotion and took the stuff. It did not do anything except make me very sleepy. Also I had had a letter to say that if I did not marry this boy he would pack up our relation-ship and find someone else, and when he came back from Singapore that is just what he did do. He married a girl he had known before me. My mother and father were quite overjoyed about this.

I was given more work at nights to do, and on Sunday he would get me out of bed at 5 a.m. to chop wood and then he used to go on his jaunts round the pubs. He soon picked up with a lady friend and once when I went to the pictures with my mother in E— Road we were coming back on the underground and who should we see behind us on the same escalator but my father and a woman. Well, we got to the top of the escalator and I said to him, 'Who is the lady?' and he told me to mind my own business and was drunk and grabbed hold of my hair and dragged me along the road to Tottenham Court Road police station and he asked the police to take me and put me away as he said he did not want me, but the police told him to take me home and if he did anything cruel to me again they would lock him up, so he was forced to do as he was told.

I remember when I was at school he used to come home drunk and he could not walk up the stairs, he used to walk on all fours and he used to get me in the corner of the room and punch me on my head and say, 'Why were you born?' Well, I have often wondered why, myself . . .

Anyway after the break-up I left Woolworths and went into an electrical factory and there I met my first husband and he was a ladies' man, and I used to talk to him but I never went out with him. Well, one Christmas we had a party in this factory and he got me so drunk he took me into a store-room and raped me. I did not know anything about sex although I was eighteen years old and I thought there was something wrong with me when I never had my periods. I asked a lady where I worked and she said it seemed as if I was having a baby. Well, I was terrified then of my parents but I did try to hide it, but I kept getting sick in the mornings and my mother said to me one morning have I been with a boy? I said, 'Yes', and then she called me a slut and I said I did not want this to happen. Anyway she told my father and he nearly killed me and then my boyfriend came round to my house one night and I said I will have to marry him, and he said, 'Why should I?' and I said, 'I am going to have your baby,' and he hit me straight in the stomach and I saw pink stars and all colours. He said he will have to talk to his mother and father. Well, he did and it was decided that we should get married after all. My mother and father were not really happy about it, nor his father. We went to make the arrangements at the registry office and the day was fixed for a Saturday.

Ros's story went on and on for pages and pages. This was just about the first time she'd been given the chance to settle down quietly and get her memories and thoughts collected so her whole life's story came out.

Neither of their parents came to the registry-office wedding and both refused to put them up afterwards. Then she miscarried. She miscarried a second time after her husband had pushed her downstairs, and when she was discharged from hospital she was completely alone.

She returned to her parents but her father soon threw her out and she took to the streets and ended up at the all-night Lyons. She began taking Benzedrine, then more and more of it, and ended up in St Thomas's. When she came out of hospital she tried her parents, but her father told her not to come back.

Then she was back at Lyons and on to V P wine and Dexedrine. There she met the father of her first baby. When she took him to her parents they relented and let her stay and put him in the spare room. But when her mother found she was pregnant she got rid of her to a mother-and-baby home. By this time the baby's father was in prison for robbery and assault. Ros went to live with the family of a girl she'd met in the home, but she had to work until 10 at night as an usherette and the baby, Anthony, was left cold, unfed and uncared for by the babyminder, and he died holding her finger. Ros ended up in hospital with cystitis, malnutrition and bronchitis.

Then she came back to London and persuaded her mother to let her stay. (Her father had died in the meanwhile.) She had eighteen jobs in three months. Then Anthony's father came out of prison and soon she was pregnant again, but the man was also going with someone else. Her mother then committed her to a mental hospital. When her baby, Julie, was born she was taken away after seven days because she couldn't keep her in the mental hospital.

On and on the story went. Each time Ros was discharged from hospital the only place she had to go was her mother's and her mother did not want her. The week after she gave birth to Alan her mother took him and put him into care. Ros tried to kill herself many times. Anthony's father was again in trouble with the police and almost strangled her when she said she would tell. She pointed him out to the police when they came round again, and he got five years.

Her son Joe's father was a rough Irishman, who was fourteen years older than Ros. She couldn't work so soon after she brought Joe home, so she was beaten up. And then he took Joe away when Ros was out shopping. When he came back to her he got more and more violent and alcoholic and Ros was even more frightened.

Ros stopped writing the story because Ian had come round and talked to us for a long time. Certainly he had an awful lot of problems of his own but he was not as violent as she feared. The problem for Ros was that she reacted to all men with fear and apprehension and Ian had only to raise his voice for her to get into a hysterical state about a possible row. We tried Family Service Unit who said, after endlessly making appointments that Ros and Ian didn't keep, 'We don't think these people want help.' Same story from the Marriage Guidance Council, lots of appointments broken and we were told that if people didn't really want help there was nothing that could be done. It seemed a very strange idea that when people like these two were in such dire straits there was no effort to hold out hands to help them.

We got Ian and Ros interested in the squatters movement and they began to attend meetings together although Ros still lived with us. At that time a letter was pushed through Ian's door informing Ros that her son Alan had now reached the age of sixteen and was no longer the responsibility of the State and it was up to her to find him somewhere to live.

Ros was in a great state. What happened to her – and, I discovered, happens to hundreds of other women – is that every time her children were taken away and put into care or adopted she replaced them with another. She had had seven children in all and had almost forgotten this one altogether.

Ros contacted the social worker and the boy rang up in great excitement to see his mother, whom he could not remember, and the two half-sisters he hadn't known existed. He came one morning to 2, Belmont Terrace and I shall never forget his face when he saw his mother – worn, old beyond her years, thin, with swollen red hands, standing in the bleak little house. She cried and he tried not to.

He came to see her a few more times but really more to reassure himself that there was no future in what must have been a bright dream. I contacted the hostel and told them of her condition but they said he was already in trouble with the law and they could not cope with him. Also, they told me, he had been particularly drunk and violent within the last few weeks.

63

I then heard from another social worker about Ros's son Joe who was in trouble at school and living with his father who beat and ill-treated him: they would consider taking him away but it was difficult because the boy would rather be beaten and ill-treated than go to a home. He had been a street kid for so long that they doubted that anything other than a remand home could handle him – maybe he was better off as he was.

By this time it was the end of December and Ros left the centre to spend Christmas with Ian. In the new year – it was a difficult decision – we didn't take her back in again because we could see that Ian wasn't her problem. He was a gentle and kindly man and he couldn't be blamed for the ghosts of the men who had ill-treated Ros. Besides, it was unfair to keep the children away from him, as he was very fond of them.

I saw Ros in the Goldhawk Road a few days ago. She's still with Ian, still working in the squatters movement and still in one room.

The children of battered women cannot win. When I pieced together the story of Jennifer's nine brothers and sisters I discovered that all of them were in trouble of one kind or another. One brother was in prison and three of the other boys had done time. Some of the girls had been up for shoplifting and had been on remand. I wondered, if we had had a women's aid which could have rescued her mother from the violence thirty years ago, need these tragedies have occurred?

Jennifer lost her mother when she was twelve. The welfare decided that she was not a fit person to look after her ten children, worn as she was with constant beatings from her violent husband, so the children were spread amongst foster-parents and children's homes and the mother took to the streets and became a dosser.

Jennifer was fostered to a couple who treated her cruelly and beat and starved her. She finally ran away and got a job in a hotel where she conceived her first child and then on to London, wandering until she met another man and they had two more children. He finally left her in a ghetto block of flats owned by Hammersmith Council on the third floor by herself with three children under the age of four. No pram, no family, just a tatty flat in the hostile, friendless world of those people who are considered the garbage of our society and are thrown together to rot.

Five weeks before the fire, her electricity was cut off for non-payment and she sat in the dark with no heat, and then asked the welfare to take her children into care because she could not cope. They said it was impossible because they had no places and she struggled on, deeply in debt.

On this particular day she went to the launderette and left the children in the flat. One of the fires that may well have been illegally wired up was lethal, and maybe a child threw something on it. By the time she turned the corner of the block with the laundry, there was smoke and screaming.

Neighbours were standing outside and she could hear her children crying. She could not get into the flat because the fire was roaring and she was held down by well-meaning people. The firemen went in, but it was much too late. When the men came out they were full of hatred for her – after all, she had left her children.

The police arrived and after seeing the bodies they took her to the police station and locked her in a cell for two hours while they checked to see if she had a record. During that time they berated her for leaving her children and said she should be punished and hinted that she could get a long sentence. Fortunately for Jennifer the shock was so great she could hear them but they all seemed far away like gnats buzzing round her.

She had no record, of course, so they decanted her on to the streets late at night with nowhere to go and no one to go to. She wandered round until she found a drunk she had known who took her to her house and said she could stay. Next day Jennifer went down to the welfare and they said she was no longer entitled to any housing as she had lost her children and was now single homeless and advised her she had better not go back to the shell of her flat because the neighbours, who had never lifted a finger to help her when she needed it, were prepared to lynch her. One social worker took pity on her and straight after the inquest directed her to us.

When Jennifer came into the house she was deeply shocked. She was very slim, with long black hair, and didn't look old enough to have had three children. The coroner had taken her to identify the bodies of her three children. One of them, the baby, was merely a small plastic bag of remains but the other two older ones had burnt and blackened faces with their mouths drawn back over their teeth in an agonized grimace. She lay on her camp bed among twelve other women and children, rocking with pain, and we fed her coffee and soup and as much affection as one can communicate to anyone in that kind of agony.

Her life had been so bad for so long she showed very little emotion except for the rocking back and forth and the nightmares which left her exhausted and incontinent. We feared that she might go out of her mind, but she stayed with us and she and I talked endlessly about the children and she eventually came to the conclusion that they were better off dead, which was true.

The day of the funeral was difficult for her and we took huge loads of flowers to the grave. Her social worker turned up and we were shocked to see that if you are buried on the State you are buried in a polystyrene coffin. The three little ones were lowered into the ground but the architects of such economies had forgotten that if you plug steel handles into this sort of material, it won't hold, and it looked as if the middle child was about to be spilled at our feet. The vicar was wet and useless, but we arranged a massive mound of daffodils round the grave and took Jennifer home. It was over.

She has a job near us now and pops in from time to time. We bullied her borough into giving her a flat because they felt guilty about their neglecting her when she badly needed help; also, of course, the publicity would have made life difficult for them. But they had the final say: they refused her a grant for furniture on the grounds that the stuff in her flat was still usable, although scorched by fire. The taxpayers must be protected.

One of the dangers for Jennifer was that she should immediately replace her children with other babies and we had to talk to her for ages and offer her something real in terms of human relationships. In fact she decided to have the loop put in and eventually she took over the role of caring for the babies of new people who needed a rest.

We find that the girls of the families who come to the house tend to be passive and withdrawn, in contrast to the boys who are aggressive and destructive. However, it does not mean that the girls are any less damaged.

These accounts will show you what some of the girls felt about life in their families:

Audrey, aged eleven

I am here because my father batters my mum. My father was very cruel. He didn't buy us any clothes. When my father picked on my mother I got nervous and I couldn't get sleep and sometimes I would get very sick.

One Sunday evening my mother was combing my sister's hair and my dad picked up a big chair and he threw it and it hit my sisters. It was for my mother. Every Sunday he picked on my mother.

Regina, aged thirteen

I am here because every night when my dad said he was going out he kept saying, 'Come on out for a drink,' and Mum said 'No, I'm staying because I'm tired and want to go to bed.' He would go out and get drunk and come back in and beat my mum up with me watching and listening. He would keep it up all night so that my mum would have to get up and go into my little sister's bed, but he would come in and pull her out. When he beat up my mum, my big brother would try to stop him but my dad would push him away so he would call someone like me to help him but my dad would just shout at me to go away and then push me. During the day if any of us was playing a game and he was in a bad mood, he would say something, 'Shut up, you noisy cows,' or 'Belt up, you brats,' and if we carried on playing he would hit us and send us to bed without any supper, but Mum would sneak me up something, but if he found out he would beat my mum up again like he does every night.

One day I came in from school, I put my bag in my bedroom as usual and went into the living room. As soon as I went in my dad came in straight after me. When he saw the state of the room he said, 'Why haven't you cleaned up, you lazy cow?' I tried to tell him but he would not listen so I said to him, 'You are supposed to clean up while Mum is at work,' so he hit me and sent me to bed. When he finally made the tea I heard my sister say, 'Dad, shall I call Regina up for her tea?' and he said, 'No, I'm not feeding that lazy bitch,' so when Mum got in I told her and she gave me some chips and saveloys. A few nights after he would be beating her up again.

I came here straight after my holiday because he tried to strangle my mum and she couldn't stand it any more, so we left.

Bernadette, aged twelve

We came to Chiswick because my stepfather is terrible to my mum. He smacks her on the face and beats her up. He keeps fighting and never stops. They fought over one little plug and never live in peace. The thing is when they fight, she never fights back. She should kick him back and it will teach him a good lesson, then he might never do that again. It will teach him a good lesson now everyone is gone. He is a nut-case. He is the silliest man I ever met.

There is a high rate of incest among these families, as the man does not see himself in the role of husband/father/protector/provider of the family. When the girls grow older he turns his attention quite naturally to the nubile child – usually about the age of eight or nine – and when the girl gets to thirteen or fourteen and has other boyfriends he moves down to the next girl in the family.

The little girl who accepts her father's advances decides when she is tiny that she must survive on her own and she stays out of trouble within the family, playing both sides. She seduces Dad in his good moods – extracting money with enthusiastic wriggles – and as she gets older she realizes she can hold both parents to ransom. When she gets a direct physical approach from her father she gives in gracefully, meanwhile bewailing her fate to her mother. She now has a very real power over her father because she can always 'tell' if she wishes, and incest is considered a really abhorrent crime in our society.

The mother in this case usually recognizes that she has been usurped by her daughter. Even if the situation worries her there is little she can do as both the husband and the child will unite against her. Often with a nubile girl in the house the beatings will occur less often, and for that she is grateful.

Karen gave birth to a badly deformed child as a result of her relationship with her father. She accepted his advances from the age of nine and it continued until she left home at fifteen. When she left he turned to her eight-year-old sister and Karen first discovered this when the child came to her and said she was 'bleeding in her pants'. Karen checked and immediately realized what had happened and she tried to take it to court but the case was thrown out for lack of evidence.

All these girls learn to use their bodies for profit from a very early age. Many of them have seen their mothers raped and they have never seen gestures of affection or love between their parents, so sex is just a usable commodity and they translate relationships between men and women as purely needs to be satisfied.

In many situations where the father approaches his young daughter the child rejects him utterly and runs to her mother for protection. They both risk further beatings but unless he is drunk, when he may try to rape the child using force, he usually desists. He needs the safety of collusion because, unlike beating his family, incest has been publicly denounced for centuries.

In conversations with women the question keeps cropping up, why did they marry a man who ill-treated them? One possible answer is that it is a way of coping with the confusing blend of guilt and compassion that has built up over the years of living with an uncaring or unkind or violent parent. This is true of both men and women.

The good/bad confusion of the relationship leaves no peace within the child. When the parent is good the child feels guilty for the hatred it feels during the periods when the parent is bad. This is further complicated by strong feelings of compassion and pity because the parents look helpless and in need of the child's love and affection. When the parent is bad the child becomes full of hatred and contempt for the parent and for himself for being fooled yet again by compassion. All these huge and powerful emotions are raging inside and have been roused in a child of two or three and continue right through his life. An ordinary childhood would certainly contain some of these emotions, but the child would cope with them if surrounded by a reasonable degree of love and security.

The older girl of the family has to take most of the burden of the children. After many years of beating, the mother becomes more and more broken down and her daughter, at the age of twelve or thirteen, becomes a household drudge at the expense of her education. We notice this in the bigger families that come into Women's Aid – The miniature adult who has taken the cares and responsibilities of a home and family on her shoulders from a very young age.

When the young girl has spent sixteen years of caring for a family, coping with a difficult and dangerous father – bearing in mind it is this girl who calls the police or the doctor, alerts the neighbours, nurses her mother after a beating, protects the children and gets them out of the way – it makes sense that as she turns away from the family circle she may find ordinary relationships with normal boys unfulfilling. It doesn't take long for her to find a young damaged man to care for. She may go into nursing and marry him from the hospital, which is perhaps why we see a lot of nurses coming through. Among the middle classes we see a high percentage of doctors' wives that are battered. It may be that the exaggerated need to care or go into caring professions affects both boys and girls who possess the experiences of suffering but not the emotional maturity to cope with the suffering of others.

Chapter 4

The Child is Father
to the Man

IT'S very noticeable that the boys' behaviour differs from the girls'. We've never had a school ask us to remove one of our girls because they were too violent to cope with. All the damage to our house and to the neighbours' houses is done by the boys. They have broken down the walls and keep over-running the neighbouring gardens. Exasperated neighbours ring up to complain when puppies are stoned. I can't blame the children as I know the sort of background they have experienced, but I would not like to have us as neighbours and we are lucky they are so tolerant.

We do not have the money to employ enough staff at Women's Aid to cope with the children, but those we have are excellent. We have built up a group of men and women who are dedicated to the children and understand their problems. It was very important to find good, gentle, loving men to work with the children. It is painful to see the new children flinch when they see a man in the corridor or in their playroom. Many of them run screaming into the safety of the bedrooms. Thanks to many of the men who now work with us the children are discovering that a man can hug and kiss and be hugged and kissed and also can accept a child's anger without responding with even greater violence.

Jeanne, our playgroup leader, takes both the loving and hating boys. Usually she is cross-questioned by them about her married life and they find it amazing when she says she has never been beaten.

The very badly disturbed children need hours spent with a friendly ear and loving arms to help sort out their tangled feelings. Fred (aged four) thought he was a dog when he arrived and clung fiercely to me, whimpering loudly. We used to transfer

71

him from one pair of arms to another for months. He had been badly beaten and terrorized by his father, who hallucinated, and the only member of the family that escaped beating was the dog, so Fred very wisely mimicked its behaviour. He didn't communicate with anyone except by whimpering, but after months of kissing and cuddling he slowly began to talk and play with the other children.

Wayne was three and a half when he and his mother came to us because she had been knifed in the head by her husband. Both Wayne's parents used to beat him. When you put your arms round Wayne he would respond by kicking and punching, spitting and scratching, because that was the only behaviour he'd learnt. He expressed his emotions with violence and not with caresses because that was all he'd seen. Now after months of loving care from Jeanne in the playgroup and from the rest of the community, he can exchange a kiss for a kiss.

By the time he came to us Jim had seen his mother: thrown head-first downstairs, thrown through a plate-glass window, raped, have her nose broken, kicked in the stomach, attacked with knives, thrown out of the house naked, choked unconscious and punched. At four years he had already gained the distinction of being banned from his playgroup for violence. He used to kick the walls and beat up the other children. He had a speech difficulty and he was covered in eczema, which he kept picking. He looked awful. After about a week his face cleared and the scabs began to heal, but he will still need a lot more gentle attention.

Bill is full of hate. He is already in trouble with the police at fourteen. One of the things that makes him violent is the times he tells friends of his dreadful family situation and then when they argue they throw his confidences back in his face. I tell him how I used to unburden myself to the mothers of my friends: they would listen most sympathetically and never ask me to the house again. Rejection by 'normal' children only makes Billy feel more isolated. He is being pushed outside society.

Ever since he was tiny, James has watched his mother suffer burning with a red-hot poker, cigarettes stubbed out on her face, her legs slashed with knives and his sister beaten before it was his turn. When his mother finally decided to leave, his father made a half-hearted attempt at hanging himself from a rafter: the leather belt broke under the strain of his weight. James is nine and has been attending hospital for three years for depression. James's problem is a social problem, not a mental condition. It should be his father receiving treatment at the hospital but nobody dares tackle father. James is not a stupid child, he is just paralysed with fear, so he can barely read or write. With all his other handicaps he will carry this burden as he moves from primary to secondary education.

Like James, most of the children who come into Women's Aid are educationally backward. It is hardly surprising when you consider that every day they have to face a nightmare situation at home. The day spent at school is temporary sanctuary, but as the afternoon comes to an end they get more tense in fear of what the evening will bring.

At home they are very often the only witnesses to the battering; at school they mix with 'normal' children. Most of them learn early that the best policy is not to talk about what really happens at home. Because children need to conform they build up a fantasy about their parents which fits in with the general pattern of their friends. However, they know they can only pretend outside home and once back inside the house they are up against the violence once more. They are confused between the socializing influences at school and the anarchy at home.

For Peter and his sister Emma, school had become the most important part of their lives as you will see from reading their accounts of why they came to Women's Aid:

Peter, aged ten

This is why I came to Chiswick, because my mother was ill-treated by my stepfather and I am accustomed to it because we moved before, but I like the school because they let us play good games and at play-time we play football and on Thursday we have a games club.

I like — because we lived near the park and near to my friend and at school we play conkers.

Emma, aged fourteen

I came to Chiswick because my mother was ill-treated by my stepfather. I didn't want to come to Chiswick because I love — and my school is so nice and if I live here I would have to go to another school. We left home before but we went to live with my aunt and had to go to Alfred Sutton school. I didn't like it there and I went back home and went back to Beachwood School and I was to be back but now am in Chiswick. I hate school until I get used to it but I am sure we will be going back to —.

Pete and Emma's mother came to us when she was pregnant yet again. She'd had several children in her first marriage. Her second husband was a vicious man who beat her and all of his stepchildren. He was all right to his own. Pete was the most dangerous of all the children we've ever had in the house, and that's saying something.

You've only to watch the boys in the house to see that they are the next generation's potential batterers. Many of them are extremely violent by the age of three. By eleven they are potential criminals. Where ordinary children would have a tussle or just shout in annoyance, they fight to kill. It's just as the Jesuits said, 'Give us a boy until he is seven and we will give you the man.'

Violence goes on from generation to generation. All the men who persistently batter come from homes where they watched violence or experienced it themselves. They saw their fathers beating their mothers or were themselves beaten as children. Violence is part of their normal behaviour. They learned, as all children do, from copying what they saw, and what they experienced.

I suppose the most obvious example of the way violent men are bred by violent men is that of Dora's family. Both Dora and her daughter-in-law, Sylvia, have come to Women's Aid. Sylvia got the same kind of treatment from Dora's son as Dora had from her husband.

Take Joan's family as the most complete example of this pattern. Joan came to Women's Aid at Easter 1973. She was referred by social services because they were worried by her husband's behaviour. She had been into the court for an injunction and to petition for a divorce on the grounds of persistent cruelty. However, there was absolutely no chance of keeping her husband outside the matrimonial home. When she returned to the house with her injunction he waited until dark and then broke in and beat her up. Neighbours heard the screaming and called the police. When the police arrived they looked at the injunction and said they were very sorry but they could not arrest him. Only the tipstaff and bailiffs have the right to arrest on a High Court injunction. They work 9.30 – 5.30 p.m., Mondays to Fridays. She would have to go back to her solicitor in the morning and get back into the High Court and have him summoned for contempt. This she did and the judge told him off and warned him severely that the next time he broke in he would be sent to prison.

The next time was just two weeks later. He backed a lorry through the hedge into the front garden, threatened to set an Alsatian on to her, smashed the windows and finally got in. This time we had moved a woman in to act as a witness so he didn't get round to beating her up. In the morning Joan went back to her solicitor and he was again summoned to the High Court. It took some time for the inquiry agents to find him and serve the papers because he kept moving from address to address. When they did get him into court the judge gave him seven days' remand for psychiatric reports. When he completed his seven days the judge (a different one each time) looked at the report which said 'personality disorder', accepted his humble apology and let him go.

Joan found him waiting outside the school when she went to meet her three boys. He had told the boys, 'It's your mother's turn next.'

One day went by. The next night at 3 a.m. her husband had broken in again. This time he raped her at the point of a knife, dragged her round the room by her hair and hit her on the side of the head and burst her ear-drum. Joan went back to her solicitor, who again served papers on him, and the judge (a different one again, nor did he appear to have read the affidavit) gave him *seven days*. By this time Joan saw no point in the law, its courts and injunctions. She moved back into Women's Aid with her three boys for good.

Her husband had spent his childhood away from his parents. He experienced mindless brutalities at the school where he was brought up. There he was often tied to the verandah and whipped.

It is interesting that her husband does not confine his violence to Joan and has beaten members of his own family. Even his mother has had to take out an injunction against him.

When Joan's boys moved into Women's Aid my heart sank. They were the most angelic-looking children of ten, seven, and five, but the oldest one particularly was very violent. Any sign of frustration would reduce him to a cursing, dangerous tantrum. The middle one was very withdrawn and hung on to his mother while the younger one smiled a huge winning smile while he tripped the other kids up as they passed by.

It turned out that their father, when bored, used to smash up their house and, when really bored, would shoot down all the crockery with his air rifle. These pastimes seemed very exciting to small boys. All the neighbours were terrified of him and if, as one neighbour did, someone complained about the screams coming from the house, their windows were smashed or nasty things happened to their animals. As far as the boys were concerned, Dad was a sort of superman who could defy everyone, even the police.

The middle boy was particularly attached to his mother and her husband used to threaten to kill him to his face, which explained why the child was so withdrawn. But the youngest one was his favourite and this was the little boy who wrote me a story about why he came to Women's Aid:

I came to Women's Aid a few months ago. I came here because there is nowhere else to go. I came here because my dad keeps beating up my mum. He dragged her up the stairs by her hair. He also squashed me against the wall behind my mum. He keeps on punching her. I like my dad the same as my mum.

This is the pattern we have found: The man who is violent comes from a home where there was violence and dreadful unhappiness. He tries to compensate by creating a home of his own as soon as possible. He is charming and considerate while he is courting because he wants to get the support and comforting he never had. For the majority of girls marriage is the ultimate goal and the earlier the better, so he is usually successful. Many of the women who come to us married soon after they left school. Most married before they were twenty-four. When the beatings begin she is totally bewildered unless she herself comes from a family where she witnessed or experienced violence – then she tends to accept her role passively. Usually the first beating occurs on the honeymoon because the man is still an immature, damaged child who reacts to any stress with total explosion, and what was a temper tantrum at five is a lethal act of aggression at twenty-one.

He most often refuses to let his wife use any form of contraceptive. If she tries and is discovered she will be beaten again so she is soon pregnant. The pregnancy itself often precipitates more violent punching and kicking. Some of the babies are born brain-damaged and many prematurely.

John's mother came to us months before he was born. She was twenty-one and badly scarred from a car accident. She had been catapulted through the front window of a sports car and the damage furrowed her face and spread her nose across her cheeks. She was in hospital for three weeks and then she was moved to a mental hospital to recover from the psychological damage of the accident. There she met a sympathetic man who didn't seem repulsed by her face and they discharged themselves together and set up a home. He turned out to be a very violent man with a long history of armed robbery, and she arrived on our doorstep.

After a few weeks she found she was pregnant and went back hoping idealistically that he would change. We lost touch for a few months until she arrived with the baby. He had been beating her when the baby cried and she in turn hated the baby. John was then four months old. He screamed all the time. His body was rigid and didn't fold naturally into my arms. He seemed to be in a state of perpetual terror. His arms would wave wildly over his head and his eyes would roll at the slightest noise. He kept pushing his bottle away. He distrusted everyone and everything. His mother said she would throw him out of the window. We telephoned social services and asked them if they could foster the baby for a while. 'We don't approve of babies of that age being separated from their mothers,' I was told. Stuff them – we don't approve of babies being thrown out of windows. Both John and his mother needed peace. We found a warm, motherly woman who took John over and his mother slept for three days. Unfortunately, her husband found us and he terrorized her with threats and she finally in panic went back to him. They collected the baby from the foster mother. We will see her again and I hope we can offer her more than six feet of floor space.

The baby spends the first days in the safety of the hospital and then goes home. One of the first problems is that the father cannot tolerate the baby crying. Crying makes him feel bad because of his own violent experiences in childhood. So when the baby cries he feels violent and lashes out at the mother with an order to keep the baby quiet. The new-born baby is aware that the mother is tense and irritable and so continues to cry. The father threatens the mother that if the baby is not silenced he will hit her. The child is now in great danger because under the strain the mother may eventually become violent towards the child. She may shake the baby or put a pillow over his face because she is terrified that she may be beaten yet again.

Some babies don't survive: two die violent deaths every day of the year. Those that survive a violent infancy may be physically tough, but they are psychologically damaged. Whatever happens, the child can't win. If he forms a good relationship with his mother, that may turn his father against him.

The child that is the most able survivor is the potential batterer in the next generation. This child learns to cut off from both parents and look after himself. He becomes 'affectionless'. He relates to everyone. He is popular, cheerful, and cheeky while he is young. When he get older his cheek turns to aggressive rudeness. His gregarious nature irritates because he uses it to manipulate and he usually sides with his father and despises his mother. His father is the strongest member of the family and also is the source of cash. He begins to treat his mother like his father does.

He precipitates rows and finds it easier to hate his mother than cope with the pain of being unable to defend her. This child goes through life perpetually in trouble. His path through school is peppered with complaints from teachers. He lies, he cheats and he steals. However, he is forgiven many of his misdemeanours because of his clear eyes, engaging smile and promises to reform. This child comes into Women's Aid and settles in immediately. He is violent only when crossed and then he is very violent; however, he can usually use his violence to gain an end so even in the midst of an explosion he has control and he watches the effect it has on those around him.

Obviously, each child reacts to the family situation according to his temperament. The boy who grows up very close to his mother feels the pain of what is happening to her very intensely. He is helpless when the beatings start, and as many of the husbands insist on the children watching he will stand watching, then throw himself in, trying to pull the father off. This is often when he will get attacked. This child is in a quandary because his feelings for both his parents are alive and painful. He identifies with his father as the man of the family and at times the father behaves like a normal father.

At least on television or in the cinema the child sees a goodie and a baddie and can identify the goodie, who still tends to win in the end. At home Dad is both goodie and baddie and the child feels the powerful conflict of both loving and hating at the same time. It is difficult enough for a normal child to cope with his conflicting feelings for his parents but it is impossibly damaging for a small child to cope with the bitter hatred for his father after a serious beating and then the remorseful approach that often occurs a few hours later. Children are endlessly forgiving towards their fathers and their love is as real and as strong as those children who have a good father.

This child comes into Women's Aid clinging to his mother, worried and anxious. When he is under stress he loses all control and he explodes and lashes out, usually falling to the floor, kicking and banging his head. He has to be prised away from a child he is attacking, or even the staff. Quite often a child will tell me that he feels 'real' when he explodes and not real when he is under control in his everyday life.

It is hardly surprising that this child grows up into the man who explodes when he is frustrated. At an age when small children are learning about society and how they are expected to respond to the demands made on them by the world they live in, they have learned a pattern of response fromt heir fathers who solve all problems with their fists. If something annoys and upsets them their response is to annihilate it. Dad can outwit the courts and all the neighbours fear him. He is all-powerful.

Many of the men who batter have already been diagnosed as mentally ill, but the machinery of the Mental Health Act is often operated by people who appear to insist that only death will part marital partners. For the woman who wrote this letter it almost came to that:

Nottingham

For eighteen years I and my two children suffered from violent attacks from my husband. Eventually he was arrested and charged with causing grievous bodily harm after beating me with the metal tube of a vacuum cleaner. Until the Mental Health Act is altered these tragic cases will continue. My husband was certified five times and although he was a border-line case he was discharged as soon as the mental health authorities considered he had recovered. Even after he had brought my nine-month-old baby to me as he thought he had strangled him, and put my other son in a bath of cold water saying the rays from the radio were burning him up. He was not to blame. Any bitterness I feel is from the fact that no one would listen and realize that he should be kept under control for the safety of the community. He is now certified for life. I am over sixty and disabled as a culmination of the injuries I received.

This is not an isolated case. Each week we get letters from women who are living in terror with the men who have often come near to killing them.

Shrewsbury

Please can you help us. I am living in fear that I will be strangled and my two children will have no one. I have gone so far as to make a will. I have been married for thirteen years; my daughter is twelve my son two. My husband appears to go out of his mind, his face goes blue and saliva drips from his mouth, his eyes go like glass and he spits in my face and gets me by the throat. He has done this for the past three years. Before that he would kick and throw me around. He has been in a mental home last year and he was at his mother's when he had something come over him and the doctor had him sent away. After this we were told it was a clash of character so my husband would not go to see the doctor again.

I have tried to help as much as possible but he is getting worse. He made a mess of me three weeks ago. The doctor told me to go to my parents for a day or two. I went home after ten days because my parents are bedridden and the rest did not appear to help so I knew I had to go back. Then there was my daughter's school.

I have been on the council waiting list for three years and now they tell me I will never get a house until I leave him. I have tried to get rooms in the — area but it seems impossible. It is only a small place.

If this be true that we clash, how is it that he will fall over when he is out, then come home and start on me? Also at 5.30 a.m. he will wake me from sleep and punch me.

I am going downhill. Please can you tell me someone that can get me a place and get me away from this house. My parents would give me some money for a house, only it does not seem possible to get a mortgage.

Yours sincerely,

VP

Cardiff

Dear Madam,

I am in the unfortunate position of being knocked about by my husband ever since he had a type of blackout. I have tried to leave my husband but as I am originally from India (I am Anglo-Indian, my husband is British) I only have a few relations in the London area. I have found it very difficult to get separate accommodation.

On the last occasion – August 1972 – my husband had one of his violent tempers and after knocking me about he locked me out. I got the police as I suffered from asthma and my tablets were in the house. Nothing could be done and if it were not for the fact that one of the neighbours took me in I could have been out in the cold all night as my husband would not open the door to the police, so they left hoping I would be all right at my neighbour's.

I tried to get a separation but the solicitor wanted a witness and the neighbour could not come forward as her husband did not want her to become involved. Also the solicitor wanted me to get separate accommodation. I tried to get the council to see if they would put the house in my name but this was not possible and so after a long and uneventful effort, I gave up trying as the strain and worry of looking after the four boys (aged twelve, eleven, nine and six) under the circumstances made me very ill. My husband promised the children and me that he would never do it again.

In the early part of this year he tried to choke me and held on to my throat until I was not aware of what was happening. My husband is very irresponsible and leaves me to manage on the bare minimum and if anything goes wrong with his money, he takes it from the housekeeping. I get £20 sometimes and at others less. After paying everything I have nothing left for emergencies. My husband goes out quite often and smokes heavily and he never goes short of anything but the minute I ask for a proper amount of housekeeping, i.e. when he deducts some out of £20, he knocks me about. He used to be ten times worse when I was pregnant. I have a handicapped girl in — Hospital and as a result I was sterilized as I was beaten right through pregnancy.

The children are much older now and my fourth child screams when he attacks me. He promises not to do it again but once he starts he does not know when to stop.

Last night he punched me across the mouth and cut my lip, which is black and blue, and he cut the back of my head. He has been wasting the money and keeping us short so I asked him about it and that was the result. He is the worse for drink and he also sleep-walks and leaves all the lights on when he is drunk. I cannot speak to him at all because he is so violent. I dread the nights when he goes out drinking and comes back drunk.

I have to work full-time and am a shorthand typist. I stick it here because of the children or else I would leave.

Any help and advice from you will be greatly appreciated.

Sussex

I just want to say how pleased I am that at last the plight of the battered wives and their unfortunate offspring is being brought out into the open. What does amaze me is that this type of man is allowed to remarry, after all if one is found guilty of ill-treating a dog, they are forbidden to keep a dog for so many years, and quite rightly so.

I was married to a homicidal maniac for nineteen years. Not only was he cruel to me, he was also cruel to the children. He also kept me short of money and as a result I was forced to go out to work when the youngest child was eighteen months old; not that I was any better off because whilst I was earning a wage he gave me little or no money at all. I obtained two legal separations for persistent cruelty and failure to maintain, and eventually a divorce on the same grounds.

During each of my pregnancies he made a point of deliberately kicking me in the stomach but thank God they were at least all born normal, certainly no thanks to their father.

On several occasions I was compelled to go to the police and I must confess that on the whole they were sympathetic and understanding, but one or two of them found the whole thing amusing. Believe me, it is not funny. I was desperate. My doctor knew about this ill-treatment but when asked to give evidence on my behalf at the divorce hearing he refused on religious grounds.

I was informed by the welfare officer just before my divorce that I could have asked the N S P C C for help as they would have made him keep us, but how is one to know these things without being told? I feel sick every time I think that some poor woman might be going through the same ill-treatment. He hated the children to such an extent that I was not allowed to knit or sew for them in front of him. He even begrudged them the time I took to bath them as babies. Also another amazing factor was that he could not bear to see anything belonging to the children in the house; he would throw toys, clothes and anything anywhere as long as it was out of his sight. There was never allowed to be anything to remind him that children were in the house. There was no doubt in my mind that he was a sick man and in need of treatment, but that was no consolation to me because unless he volunteered to go into hospital for treatment, which he refused to do anyway, no one could force him to. I do know that he remarried and that his wife left him. I also know that he lived with two other women, both of whom walked out on him, so you see he has obviously still got his sadistic streak and no doubt always will have.

It has sometimes seemed as though one of us at Women's Aid will have to be killed before anyone will take the situation seriously. At the house we are constantly threatened by angry husbands, and some of them are armed. The police don't come round fast enough to protect us. They are over-worked, as usual, and resent the fact that by the time they do arrive some of the men have run off. We have had our windows smashed so often that we now have perspex screwed over the front ones, which cost about £300. Ideally I would have liked the new bullet-proof glass installed but that would have cost £2,000 and we haven't got it, so the perspex will have to do.

Only once has a husband broken into the house, but we were really lucky that he wasn't carrying a knife. The day Esmond broke in started normally, but very soon someone said, 'Lee's husband is outside.' Lee ran upstairs to the top floor and barricaded herself in with the children. He came to the front door four times. We tried to reason with him and asked him to make an appointment through his solicitors but we realized that it was useless because he was having hallucinations. He was convinced he was God and had come to kill the dragon because he was ordered that this should be so.

Ten minutes after he first came, someone went into the office to telephone the police. Suddenly huge lumps of concrete arrived through the large front windows. Glass shattered everywhere – some of the blocks narrowly missed the babies asleep in their cots upstairs. Then there was a silence. Ten minutes went by. The police station is only a few hundred yards up the road.

Then a crash sounded through the house. Esmond had thrown himself, feet first, through the basement window. Many of the women panicked and screamed. The children were not terrified at all. Jenny, Pat, Anne and John Ashby fought with him and stopped him at the first floor. He roared and ranted and screamed that he would kill Lee and he had the strength of ten.

I collected as many of the children as I could find and herded them into the playgroup downstairs. I then shut the basement door and stood in front of it with an empty bottle of orange squash in one hand and tried to look resolute.

Upstairs I could hear them struggling with him. It seemed to go on for ages and then he broke loose and came running down the corridor towards me. He skidded to a stop and we looked at each other and then he turned and ran upstairs. I don't think it was the calmness of my gaze. I am a very big woman and it probably saved me from a nasty fight. We managed to restrain him and got him out of the house. He came in again through the basement window and again we got him out.

Twenty minutes after we'd called for them the police arrived in a panda car. They picked him up and took him away.

His small daughter was so disturbed by her father's visit that she started to bite again, just when she was getting better. She got into one of the babies' cots and savaged it so badly that the baby had to be taken to hospital. The community discussed the whole situation and everybody restrained themselves from lashing out at Cherie as they clutched their bleeding offspring to their bosoms. She did settle down again after a few weeks.

Esmond got three months for the damage to the house and did his time in the medical wing of Wormwood Scrubs. He kept on hallucinating. He used to smash up his room and everything in it because he was afraid of evil spirits which controlled his mind and body. Part of his problem is that he has no family and no relations here. He wants very much to go back home to his own country and all his relations. So we asked Neville Vincent for the money for an air ticket, but the flight was due out a few days after his prison sentence ended and by that time he had become the responsibility of the psychiatric unit of Hackney Hospital. The psychiatrist there didn't think he was suffering from mental illness. Esmond was taken to the airport, but he didn't fly out. Everyone thought a male nurse was necessary but no one would authorize the expense of a male nurse to accompany him to Guyana. He is still in Hackney Hospital. He writes fond letters to Lee which make her cry but she knows she can't go back – it would be too dangerous. Yet he can discharge himself at any time and turn up on her doorstep.

Some of the men who batter are alcoholics, but stopping them drinking doesn't stop the violence. Anything can release the trigger of violence in a batterer. It can be alcohol, a child crying, or a bad day on the horses. With most it is not one blow and have done – they never seem to let up hitting once they've started. They just keep going on and on with fists, feet, furniture, anything that comes to hand. This fourteen-year old boy has watched his mother being beaten for as long as he can remember:

We came to Chiswick Women's Aid because my dad beat up my mum. He used to punch her and when she fell to the ground he'd kick her in the stomach. He wasn't a good father nor he wasn't a good husband neither. We couldn't make friends, even our relations couldn't come and visit us because he'd always start a fight with them and then he'd tell them to F— off. So after twenty-three years of hell and torture my mum decided to get out and try and start new in a different environment so we came to England and we went to my mum's brother's but he only had a one-room flat so we couldn't stay there for long so my mum went to social security. They told us to come here.

The following letters are from the Women's Aid mail-bag:

Tower Hamlets

Dear Mrs Pizzey,
I have been listening to Jimmy Young's programme and was rather pleased to know that something is being done to help us unfortunate women who are beaten. My husband has been violent towards me many times. It hasn't been as regular as some of the examples given by you but I have been bruised all over except my face. It isn't just one slap and done with, he carries on and on. It has been

particularly about the head lately and in fact I have started to suffer from dizzy spells. The last time was Sunday, when I was threatened with a knife and was nearly strangled.

It gets worse and worse in spite of all the promises, and I really would like a separation, but how do you find a place to live with four children?

My husband said he would never let me have the children if I left. How do I stand there?

Looking forward to hearing from you.

No address given

Dear Madam,

I have been reading about your good work you are doing for these poor unfortunate wives. I'm writing to you because I was one of those wives but I had both violent cruelty and mental cruelty, but my husband said to me, 'I will never mark you,' so I got punched around the head and he used to torment me by making me have sex three or four times a night, kept me awake night after night rowing over this, and in the finish I went into hospital. I am only thirty-nine and the sister in the ward said I was worn out. I looked like a woman in her sixties.

I nearly went out of my mind. I went to court five times before I got my separation and the only bit of luck I had was when I happened to get two tiny rooms. I had two children and one had asthma and the other suffers badly from nerves as they used to lie in bed and listen to us. No one ever gave me any help so you see I feel sorry for those wives and I know some now that are being driven mental by their husbands. They have to put up with it all because they cannot find a place to go. I stuck it for ten years but if there is a terrible tragedy in these unhappy homes the welfare step in, then of course it is too late. Who will suffer then? The children, of course.

Scotland

Dear Madam,

Having listened to the last two minutes of your interview on Radio 2 and having read the article in the *Daily Mail*, I felt compelled to write to you. I am an ex 'battered wife' and have finally left my husband with my daughter who is nine months old. She was born with a congenital dislocation of the hip. She was being treated in — where I come from and the decision to interrupt her treatment was a very difficult one to make, despite my desire to leave the horrors of being married to a nightly wife-beater and an alcoholic.

I will not go into the details of the terrible cruelty that I have suffered although I would be more than willing if they would be of any use to you.

My husband is a *general practitioner* and whilst at medical school was an amateur boxer, so he had plenty of brawn as well as brain, plus enough money to keep him well supplied with as much whisky as he wanted.

I have left him four times previously but always ended up going back to him because he would find out where I was – usually with my elderly parents – and harass and threaten them at all hours of the day and night, at the same time promising to mend his ways and pleading with me to go back because he loved me.

He is an excellent doctor and a much-respected public citizen. He was, however, on his own insistence, my own doctor and treated me with utter contempt even when I threatened to miscarry at twelve weeks of pregnancy, and also during and after my baby's delivery. (I gave birth to her at home without a midwife present.)

This last time, having made the decision to get away and stay away, regardless of the consequences, I was fortunate in that my brother and his wife, whom I had not seen for years, suddenly stepped in and offered me accommodation in their small flat. I am a qualified teacher and now have a job, an excellent solicitor and a very understanding GP.

I have been away now for two months and after experiencing the immediate relief of no more mental and physical cruelty, I am now trying to adjust to a very uncertain future, accompanied by continual nightmares and depression.

I always felt I had no one to turn to, my family lived a long way away and I was too ashamed to tell friends who all thought the world of my husband.

I often sat and thought, 'If only there were someone to turn to, somewhere to go.'

I am lucky in that I have a strong personality and also have kind relatives and the knowledge of how to go about getting supplementary benefit, I have a good solicitor who is working hard to try and get me a legal separation and custody of my child as quickly as possible.

I believe that Women's Aid is absolutely essential for women like myself who have no alternative to staying at home and putting up with all that it entails, appealing to disinterested friends, distant relatives, the unsympathetic council for accommodation, or the social services.

I believe it needs enormous determination (and some women after years and years of cruelty by battering have had all their determination knocked out of them) firstly to make a break and secondly to stick to it, once one realizes that, from now on, 'You are on your own.' One has to face the fact that one has to be mother, father, breadwinner and housekeeper alongside the continual terror, in my case of being discovered by my husband and assaulted yet again. I cannot forget the nightmare existence of my past nor can I face the thought of being regarded as an oddity – an outcast almost – by a society which in general has absolutely no conception of the 'battered-wife' syndrome.

I do hope we can meet some time and I certainly hope I can help you.

In our experience many of the men have little insight into their behaviour. In the film *Scream Quietly* Kath described how when she was out with her husband they saw a man punching up a woman. Her husband remarked, 'Look at that, isn't it disgusting?' When Kath said, 'Well, that's what you do to me,' he replied, 'That's different, you're my wife.'

They are prepared to go to any length to make their wives feel guilty at having left them. Many are unwilling to be divorced by their wives and apply for custody of the children – this even after they have used their belts on their children in the street. Others take to drink, and go on the road. Some attempt suicide. There are five overdoses at the moment: some are pretty puny with their intention – they take twenty junior aspirin – but one has put two air-gun pellets into his head. Others put on an act of utter repentence and are perfectly convincing to people who'd like to be convinced. One of my more bizarre conversations was with Lesley's social worker. She telephoned to say that Lesley's husband was terribly sorry, would she come back? I said, 'But he threw scalding water over her and gave her second-degree burns on her breasts.' 'Oh yes, yes, I know,' she said, 'but he's terribly sorry.'

Those who recognize the mechanism – that the man will be charming to get what he wants, and turn off the charm fast if he's frustrated – are cynical about his contrition, as this ten-year-old girl told about her father: 'He said that he wouldn't do it again, but it was the same old story.'

Helen, aged thirteen

We came to Chiswick Women's Aid because nearly every night my dad came home and demanded his dinner. He also kept saying that my mum was going out with boyfriends. One night my mum and dad were fighting when I was in bed so I got up and ran straight to the police station. They brought me home in a car and warned him not to do it again. Then we left him when he was at the dog track and we went to Scotland but we was only there a few weeks when he came again and said that he wouldn't do it again, but it was the same old story.

The next night I was at home with my dad because my mum took my sister and brother to Scotland and just in spite he went out to the pub nearly every night and left me at home. I went round my nan's but they said he's entitled to go out because my mum does. But my mum has never gone out and left us.

Another night when my mum was away I let the bird out but he just laid in the bed so I had to run round my nan's at 12 o'clock at night and had to bring my grandad round. I wished that some day he could go into a mental home.

It's a rare and generous man who repents and says, 'There are letters, words like mine in almost every man, most of us are too tongue-tied, *ashamed* and stupid to express them, especially to the ones we've harmed so grievously.' This once-violent man wrote to us the evening he saw our film. I cried when I read his letter.

I heard my wife speak with many voices during your programme. Each time re-emphasized for me the shame and remorse which I used to experience *after* the madness of an incident of violence: the renewed determination of 'never again'. My sense of compassion or wisdom used to black out and die in an explosion of frustration in the moment *before* the blow was struck, just as her compassion and wisdom must have died in the moment of final provocation. What made it so reprehensible was that we were otherwise two 'normal', fairly rational and reasonable persons and apparently each capable of expressing ourselves, understanding and getting on well with almost anyone on earth except, sometimes (and not even the most *important* times!), each other.

Our three children are now scattered and unsure where 'home' really lies, although, except for our youngest who is fifteen, the elder two are fortunately old enough and mature enough to be leading their own lives and making their own careers and decisions. My wife (it's difficult to learn to precede 'wife' with 'ex' or 'former'!) lives a kind of gypsy life in the hotel trade living in the company of another man. I live alone, very much withdrawn and with few visits from children or friends, with remembrances as punishments far more numerous than consolations. That I am deprived of making direct atonement is in itself the greatest punishment.

Heart-failure in 1972 and two heart-attacks with three months in hospital recently have warned me that I may be running out of time to do much or anything to try to make amends (agnostic, I can't even get religion!) and disablement benefit doesn't leave much cash to afford charitable gifts. On the other hand, I cannot afford *not* to send a pound to help you because it is the behaviour of men like me who cause the need for your work and even though I know that a million pounds cannot compensate for one blow struck or ever properly say 'I'm sorry', still, I think you will understand what I'm trying to do and why?

You will probably also understand what it was last September which brought my wife racing from — to my hospital in — to see me when my 'clock' almost stopped. I think she feels no cause to *fear* me now; just a special kind of friendship and, I hope, some forgiveness. Selfishly, I hope she has not seen or may hear of your programme. For her it could only serve to revive memories which I would wish her to forget.

Yours very sincerely,

He later wrote to me, 'One single act of violence is as damaging, creates as much lasting fear, impresses a watching child, as a hundred years of repetitive acts.' It's the children who suffer and they grow up to make their own children suffer and the pattern repeats through each generation. The answer is simple – rescue this generation of children from learning violence. But when has public money ever been spent before the event? For generations the established charities and more recently the State social welfare services have been picking up the pieces after each individual family crisis. They've not asked or looked for the cause of the troubles or done anything to eradicate them.

Chapter 5

Problem –
What Problem?

IT would probably take a Charles Dickens to do full justice
to the labyrinth of indifference, red tape, callousness, and
simple incompetence that exists between people in need and so
many of the agencies that are meant to help them from the
DHSS to the NSPCC.

The women and children who end up at Women's Aid are
living evidence of just one corner of that maze. They show that
when a woman tries to gather herself and her children away from
the muggings of a brutal husband, she can limp to her GP,
stagger to the casualty ward, drag herself to the social worker,
cry out to the police, beseech the Marriage Guidance Council,
implore the Family Service Unit, plead with Dr Barnardo's,
beg the NSPCC and come away, through the swish of hands
being compassionately washed in all directions, with only a
babble of conflicting advice and not one jot of practical
help.

5,500 women have come through Women's Aid so far, and
every one of them adds evidence to the case that says the agencies
which we might like to believe in as proof that ours is a humane
society simply do not work. This chapter looks at some of the
main agencies and how they fail.

In the rush of coping with so many cases in two and a half
years, documentation at Women's Aid has sometimes been
erratic. But 270 cases that I did manage to record in detail
over one period give an idea of how widespread are both
battering and official failure to deal with it. Incidentally in
sixty-seven of those cases it wasn't just the mothers who were
battered but the babies and children as well.

The cases were referred to Women's Aid by the social
services, the police, the probation service, the Citizens' Advice

Bureaux, St John's Ambulance, doctors, hospitals, the Samaritans, Shelter, the N S P C C and the press.

Amersham	1	East Ham	1	Isleworth	2
Archway	1	East Molesey	1	Islington	5
Ashford	1	Edinburgh	1		
		Edmonton	1	Kensal Rise	1
Barnet	1	Essex	5	Kew	2
Bermondsey	1			Kingston	1
Birmingham	2	Farnborough	1		
Bolton	1	Feltham	2	Lambeth	2
Bow	3	Flintshire	1	Lewisham	1
Brent	2	Fulham	10	Limerick	4
Brentford	3			Liverpool	4
Bristol	1	Glamorgan	1		
Brixton	2	Gloucestershire	1	Maida Vale	1
		Greenock	1	Maidenhead	1
Camberwell	4	Greenwich	1	Manchester	1
Camden	2	Grimsby	1	Mile End	1
Canning Town	1			Monmouthshire	1
Catford	1	Hackney	3		
Chatham	1	Hammersmith	26	Newcastle	1
Chelsea	5	Hampstead	1	New Cross	1
Chippenham	1	Hanwell	1	Norfolk	2
Chislehurst	1	Harlesden	1	Northolt	1
Chiswick	11	Harlington	1	Norwood	2
Clapham	1	Harringay	1		
Clapton	2	Harrow	2	Oxford	1
Cobham	1	Havering	1		
Covent Garden	1	Hayes	2	Paddington	3
Coventry	1	Heston	1	Peckham	1
Croydon	1	High Wycombe	2	Penge	1
		Holborn	1	Poplar	1
Dagenham	1	Holland Park	4	Putney	2
Dartford	1	Hornsey	3		
Dublin	3	Hounslow	1	Reading	1
Durham	2	Huntingdon	1	Redditch	1
				Reigate	1
Ealing	8	Isle of Dogs	1	Richmond	1

St Albans	2	Sutton	1	Watton at Stone	1
Sevenoaks	1	Swanscombe	1	Wembley	2
Sidcup	1			West Kensington	1
Slough	1	Teddington	1	Whitton	1
Southall	5	Tottenham	3	Willesden	1
Southend	1	Tower Hamlets	3	Wimbledon	1
Southward	4	Twickenham	1	Wolverhampton	1
Stanmore	1			Wood Green	3
Stepney	1	Wadhurst	1	Woolwich	1
Stoke Newington	1	Walthamstow	3		
Sunderland	1	Wandsworth	4	Yorkshire	1
Surbiton	1	Watford	2		

Now let's look at some of the agencies who referred these cases to Women's Aid, and who still are referring cases, and see how they fail.

Social Services

The motive behind the work of all family case-work organizations is the support and strengthening of the family. A battered wife struggling to break away from a disastrous marriage can expect little sympathy from a social worker, and in many cases she will experience downright hostility.

The social worker is trained to consider both sides of a marital problem, which is normally a just and fair approach, but where the woman is being savagely beaten it seems hardly reasonable to pause and weigh the merits of the case.

In the majority of cases where a battered woman presents herself at the social services she will be told that there is nothing that can be done for her because (a) she is technically not homeless, as she has a home to go to and a husband to maintain her, and therefore she is not the responsibility of the State; and (b) the social services cannot make a moral judgement on a marriage: By that they mean that they don't want to take sides – and giving a wife refuge presupposes guilt on the part of the husband. However, it never occurs to them that by refusing her refuge they presuppose that the husband is innocent.

The only real offer of help she will get is an offer by the social worker to visit the husband. This puts her in a dilemma because if she agrees and goes home after the social worker has visited him he may well beat her severely for putting him in a humiliating situation. Many is the husband who has promised total reform to a social worker only to round on his wife and black both her eyes half an hour later.

It always amazes me to hear a social worker telephone and say, 'Mr Jones has promised never to hit his wife again and I feel she should give it another try.' In that particular case the woman had been married for nineteen years. She had been battered so badly that her face looked like a ploughed field and both the children had been beaten ever since they were born. Women's Aid was the first place that had offered her refuge in all that time. She had tried to get away many times and her case was well known in her area. Yet here was the social worker who knew the husband and his reputation and even admitted that he was frightened of him, saying that on the strength of a promise he advised this woman to go home. How any social worker believes that a man who has been violent for years can just suddenly stop overnight is beyond me. I feel that most social workers know very well that the man is not going to change, but when the wife has moved away they become the recipient of some of the man's aggression. Many of the husbands do make a menace of themselves, particularly if they believe the social worker knows where their wife is and is not telling them. Some social workers don't bother to keep it a secret. They give the husband our phone number or address, thus removing the burden from their own shoulders.

As most of these husbands have been violent since well before they married, it is hardly fair to insist that the problem lies within the marriage. But the social worker, trained or brain-washed into this limited form of thinking, will continue to plaster over the cracks, telling the mother that her husband is ill and needs her and that she must stay for the good of the children. This last comment is made in spite of overwhelming evidence from school, neighbours, etc., that the children are being severely damaged in the situation.

As social workers mostly deal with problem families they have come to accept that violence amongst their clients is the norm.

They will produce arguments to prove that an uneducated man who beats his wife is showing an inarticulate form of love for her. When you point out that wife-battering is not a working-class syndrome and is spread right through society, they are amazed. This is because they have probably never come across a middle-class woman asking for help.

Social workers must learn to respect the woman they are there to help. Too many accept that beatings are a part of life and urge women to put up with them. Every time the mother turns up at the social services she is told that nothing can be done except to have her children taken into care. This is a terrible trap to fall into.

Once she agrees in desperation to hand over the children, she is then no longer considered a family. On her own without children she can probably find a bedsitter, but to get the children back she must find suitable family accommodation. But because she no longer has the children in her care she cannot be considered for council accommodation, so she faces the usually impossible task of finding and paying for a family house in the open market. Usually she loses the children for good except for visits. Then, all too often, nature takes over and she replaces them with yet more children.

Social workers who offer to take the children into care are well aware of these consequences but they don't ever warn the mother and they don't consider the inhumanity of depriving the children of the one parent that does love them.

Many social workers are angry and upset over the problems of battered wives but few take any steps to alter the situation. These problems have been allowed to exist for years in a supposedly sophisticated and caring welfare state. All social workers stand condemned by default because they knew and did nothing about it.

Social services have referred cases to Women's Aid from all over the country but none has ever paid us a penny for taking the mothers in. Hammersmith, who are one of our biggest customers, promised to pay but ignored our bills. Ealing, our second biggest customer, agreed that we took their families but said that as we were *persona non grata* they were unable to contribute to the cost. We have always been in a difficult position because the mothers matter far more than the money. When a social worker says that unless we take the family he will be forced to send them home we ask for money even though we know there is no chance of getting it – but we always take in the family.

Sometimes the social worker packs the family into a taxi and sends them off to us. The mother arrives with a piece of paper in her hand with our address but no idea of the social worker's name – some social workers make a point of not mentioning their name. Once the mother has spent the night in our boruogh the social workers from the original area can and do refuse to have any more to do with her because she has technically moved out of their area and thus lost all rehousing rights. Our borough quite rightly resents this approach because they now have some 200 extra mothers and children in Chiswick joining the already lengthy queue for housing.

It seems ridiculous that social services and social security are run from separate buildings because they are inextricably entwined. Instead of hand-in-hand policy between the two departments a rivalry exists and if, for example, a mother has had her gas and electricity turned off for non-payment, social services will argue that social security should pay part of the bill, and both sides will haggle while the mother sits in the cold and dark with her children.

Social workers are bound by all sorts of cumbersome rules and tied in official red tape. A major problem is that their only way towards better pay and job prospects is up the administrative ladder, so you soon lose the really gifted, humane social worker who has a family and a mortgage and cannot survive on the disgustingly low pay given to the field-workers. Within a few years he can be found with a long title, pushing an administrative pen for more money but less job-satisfaction and at the expense of the people who really need his skill and talent.

One bright ray of hope are the new community workers who are seconded to Women's Aid for a three-month training period. These people come from North London Polytechnic, LSE, Chiswick Poly and other places. They have been trained in community work and they are the future for the social services. They don't see themselves as some sort of guardians of society's conscience and handers-out of advice and bounty from above. They are moving away from the old idea that help from the social services is of an advisory nature and towards the idea that what the majority of people need is practical help to solve immediate problems.

I would like to see the present social services dissolved. In the place of these offices full of desks, typewriters and instructions in triplicate there should be large community houses with area social workers coming in daily to talk with the people who come in for advice or for a cup of coffee or to see the health visitors. The administration can be carried on in the Town Hall but the actual records kept on the clients could be reduced to a bare minimum.

At the moment there is little point in trying to get hold of a social worker in the morning because he will be in a meeting. These meetings go on all morning and then there is lunch and then he goes out to do his visits. This means that most of his clients who do not have telephones must lurk surrounded by children at phone kiosks and it can take days to get through to him.

I once asked a social worker what would happen if an emergency arose during one of the meetings and the client was unable to contact her social worker. The social worker said that there was a maxim used in his office to the effect that 'If there is an emergency call, ignore it for twenty-four hours and it will go somewhere else.' During the meetings the duty officer can be called to the phone, but of course he knows nothing of the case and is even less help than the social worker.

As most social workers come from a middle-class background or have been educated into middle-class prejudices, their attitudes to mothering and caring are largely inappropriate in working-class situations. Many times you will find a social worker more concerned about the cleanliness of the children than the quality of the loving, and far too ready to resort to the children's home should he feel that the mother is not coping.

Many social workers will complain that the battered mother is a slut because she is dirty and dishevelled, never stopping to think what repeated vicious assaults must have done to her personality. Instead of a helping hand the mother gets the cold glare of disgusted authority, and it is no wonder that mothers arrive at Women's Aid full of hostility towards social workers and the welfare state.

The Police

The police attitude to wife-battering reveals an understandable but unacceptable schizophrenia in their approach to violence. Imagine that Constable Upright is on his beat one night and finds Mr Batter mugging a woman in the street. Mr Batter has already inflicted heavy bruises to the woman's face and is just putting the boot in when Constable Upright comes on the scene. The constable knows his duty and does it. He arrests Mr Batter, who is charged with causing grievous bodily harm and goes to prison for ten years.

Ten years later Constable Upright is on his beat when he is sent to investigate screaming which neighbours have reported coming from the home of the newly released Mr Batter. Mr Batter is mugging his wife. He's thrown boiling water at her, broken her nose, and now he's trying for her toes with a claw hammer. When Constable Upright arrives what does he do? Does he make an arrest? Of course not.

He knocks on the door and Mr Batter tells him to 'sod off'. He tells Mr Batter that the neighbours are complaining and he wishes to see his wife. Mr Batter says they have been having a minor row and he gets his wife who is looking bruised round the face and crying. The policeman will not arrest. In one case the husband even assaulted his wife in front of a policeman but still there was no arrest. All that he did was to advise her to go to the local magistrates' court the next morning and take out a summons against her husband, but he knew that she was unlikely to do this because she would have to live in the same house as her husband while she was taking him to court.

Some policemen are sympathetic and show a degree of understanding of the battered women's predicament, but the usual attitude from the police force is one of growing hostility as they are called out again and again to the same house and each time the woman refuses to take action. Soon the family gets well known to the police station and they take their time about going round.

I think the police become immune to violence, dealing as they do with so many forms of violent crime. It is far easier to fall into the habit of thinking of the woman as an ill-deserving slut than to watch helplessly as she reappears time and again, getting more and more desperate each time.

The police never seem to feel that it is their responsibility to notify social services or the N S P C C even when it is obvious to them that the children have been beaten. Time and time again we have had arguments with police stations when a mother has been beaten up and thrown out leaving the children with the husband. Usually the man has a history of violence and is already known to the police. The mother's first place of call is at the police station, where she will be told that as far as the children are concerned, possession is nine tenths of the law and there is nothing that the police can do about getting the children out. It would seem obvious that the police station should then notify one of the caring agencies that the children are at risk. But they don't.

One night we had a call from a couple who had found a small boy down the road, crying bitterly and covered in bruises. They called the police, who took a long time coming. While they were waiting, the couple thought of phoning us. We gathered that the boy was terrified. The bruises had been inflicted by his father in a drunken rage, and he didn't want to go home. We suggested that the couple bring the boy to us for the night and we would call in the N S P C C. Unfortunately, before this happened the police arrived at the couple's home and took the child off. We checked with the police station the next day and we were told that they had simply called in the parents who had taken the boy home. Had they notified the social services? 'Of course,' came the prompt reply. I checked and they hadn't.

Social Security

This congested organ of the welfare state exists to alleviate suffering by handing out money to the poor and needy. By outlook and training the staff that sit behind the counter tend to consider that anyone coming to ask for money is shiftless and idle and to treat them accordingly. Yet the clerk at the counter is often taking home less than the families who are claiming, so they can't be blamed for being shitty sometimes.

As usual with huge organizations, too much emphasis goes on administration and too little on results. Too much money goes on the machine and too little to those it was set up to help. Large sums are spent on snooping and prying in order to catch the relatively minuscule number of people who are cheating, thereby proving to the public that social security is mindful of its duty as guardian of the public purse.

The first person a battered mother is likely to see will be the woman behind the reception desk at her local office. She will be told that they have no intention of giving her money because she has a home to go to and a husband to maintain her. Only if she can show proof that she is taking legal proceedings will they perhaps reconsider the matter.

Tears will not move them because there are usually two or three people in tears either of misery or rage at the treatment they are receiving. Small children clinging to her skirt will have no effect either. But if the hour is late enough and the mother is brave enough to refuse to leave, a payment of a few pounds may be made for a place for the night.

If she comes back the next day having seen a solicitor they will tell her that before she can have money for rent she must find somewhere to live and wait for a visit there from a social security officer. It is almost impossible to find somewhere to live if you cannot put down a deposit and rent in advance. Catch-22: the poor mother gives up and has to go home to violence.

Women's Aid are lucky in that we have managed to build a good relationship with our local social security branch. They are flexible and generous towards all the women who have come to us. But even they could not help us when it was decided that the total rent we could be allowed for a family, however many kids it included, would be £3.50 a week. Even the meanest hostel is subsidized £6 for each adult, plus more for each child, but we seem to get nowhere when we try to argue. This is not the fault of the local office; it is regional policy. But until voluntary bodies like us can begin to rely on an imaginative approach from social security, they may well be killed at birth by lack of funds.

What could be helpful and beneficial attempts at solving pressing social problems will wither and die.

The Department of Health and Social Security may want to think that there have been 'several developments' since we first presented a dossier to Sir Keith Joseph in summer 1972. If they've come a long way, they've got nowhere in particular.

Jack Ashley has shown me a letter from Edward Heath, who was then Prime Minister, saying that any woman who presented herself at social security and asked for help to escape from a brutal situation would immediately be given money for accommodation and food. This statement was either a bare-faced lie or a reminder that politicians and the civil servants who advise them are too often the last people to know and understand the real situation. The experiences of the women coming to the centre have proved this.

Hospitals

Hospitals have their heads buried firmly in the sand. They resolutely mutter that their job is to heal and what happens outside the hospital is no concern of theirs.

A woman married to a taxi-cab driver was rushed by ambulance with a police escort to a local hospital. The medical social worker telephoned us to say that, though she had been badly shocked, the woman would be ready for discharge after a few hours' rest, but was too frightened to go home, and would we take her? We agreed, but by the time we got through to casualty to say we would come and collect her, a doctor had persuaded her to go home and the police had driven her back.

The next morning the police telephoned me and said that she had come into the station wearing a coat over her bra and pants because she had fled from her husband after another battering. They wondered if they could bring her to us. When she arrived we were all shocked into silence. Her whole body was covered with enormous bruises and she was bleeding from several gashes. The night before when the police had returned her to the house they found that her husband had gone out, locking the door.

The police had forced an entry and left her there. Later the husband came back drunk and beat her.

I talked to one orthopaedic surgeon in a hospital, who calmly agreed that he often repaired a woman's nose five or six times at vast expense to the public and a great deal of discomfort to herself, but he did not see it as part of his job to question how her recurrent injuries were inflicted.

I often find a reluctance on the part of the staff of the hospital to confirm any diagnosis that might cause them to be called to court to give evidence, or to take any steps that might involve them in controversy. In one case, a three-month-old baby was admitted to hospital after a blow to the side of the head which made him vomit continuously and made it necessary to insert tubes to drain fluid from the brain daily. The hospital would not confirm that the blow was relevant to the fluid collecting, even though this would have been one way of getting a court injunction to keep the very violent husband away from the baby. The hospital stuck to its safe, non-committed position and merely said that the trouble could have been caused by a knock or a blow but might possibly stem from natural causes. As I write, the father is waiting to get the baby back, if it lives. He has a history of violence and is a drug-addict. It is this kind of pussy-footing that keeps the hospitals like huge ships afloat, separate from the communities that they should be serving.

If they have a difficult case to deal with they call a case conference and decide that the case is indeed difficult and by the time they all have a long chat and a cup of tea it has probably gone away in desperation.

Violence just does not occur inside nice clean and tidy hospitals. And if anyone is bad-mannered enough to show temper there are plenty of competent, cool people around to subdue him with a well-aimed needle. This was one hospital's solution to the problem of having one violent man assault his wife in the casualty ward. They took no further action.

A hospital will have no compunction in discharging a woman who has been dreadfully assaulted. A West Indian nurse arrived at Women's Aid three weeks before she was due to give birth. Her neck had been dislocated and her body was covered in scratches and bites. She was moaning and crying and we couldn't get much sense out of her. I telephoned the hospital which had put her out and asked them what they were doing, only to be told by a disapproving nursing sister that this girl was carrying another man's child. The unspoken attitude was, 'she's only got what she deserved'. A few hours later the poor woman swallowed all the pills the hospital had given her and we had her taken to another hospital. However, this was yet another case where it would be fair to say that though that extent of damage inflicted on an ordinary member of the public would have kept them in hospital for a week, because this was a woman who had been beaten by her husband she was patched up and sent out as though she somehow had deserved to be beaten.

The sooner large hospitals are no longer considered the best way of serving the community the better. The bigger they are the more impersonal they become and the easier it is for the staff to get out of touch with the people they are there to serve. In the days of small cottage hospitals there was much more care and concern for the individual.

Above all no hospital should be allowed to discharge any patient who has been a victim of assault without making sure she has somewhere safe to go to and notifying the appropriate social services.

Dora had fifteen pregnancies and ten children and the only holidays she ever had were in the maternity ward and the times she was in for injuries received from her husband. Four times the hospital had called in the priest to perform the last rites but they always sent her home to more violence. They were more concerned about the state of her soul than her body.

Mental Hospitals

A battered woman is likely to find herself in the local mental hospital on several occasions. In the majority of our cases she is admitted because she has taken so many overdoses that the local hospital is fed up with her and passes her on to the psychiatrist, who puts her into the mental hospital for 'depression'. The staff know that she has been beaten over a long period, but the matter is conveniently forgotten while she is heavily tranquillized for a few weeks, told that she is much improved, and sent home.

The psychiatrists are usually male and many hold the belief that subconsciously she needs the violence. If only she could look deep inside herself and admit her faults all would be well and her husband would not batter her any more.

This approach fills her with guilt and uncertainty. Is it her fault? She begins to wonder. It is easy to make her feel a failure when she already feels she's failed in the main purpose of her life – her marriage. She usually believes the psychiatrist and goes home determined to do better.

But she goes home to a husband whose pattern of violence was evident well before she married him and soon she is back at the mental hospital again, even more depressed. She gives up and neglects herself. She wrings her hands and cries because she has left her children at home but feels safe in the hospital and dreads going back. Meanwhile, the psychiatrist, bored with her crying, decides sometimes that the most useful move would be to perform a leucotomy and remove the anxiety.

We see the results of this operation when the women come in and recount their horrifying life histories with utter indifference. The operation does indeed remove all their anxieties and usually their children have been taken away and put into care because the mother has also lost all sense of responsibility. The husbands continue to beat them but now they put up with it with cheerful indifference. A surgical triumph?

It is sad for us because the mothers who have had this operation usually come in to ask us to help them get their children back. We feel very bitter because though they've paid a terrible price for their husbands' violence, it is far too late, and gently we have to persuade them to leave them where they are.

It is more common to see mothers who have had ECT, or 'shock treatment' as it is commonly called. Nobody really knows how or why it works but it does relieve depression. Unfortunately it also erases memory and has other side-effects if used too often. Again many of our mothers go into the mental hospital and are given a course of ECT. It helps for the moment, but they go home and are repeatedly battered until in the end you find a confused, witless forty-year-old sitting in front of you, trying to remember when and where she was last jolted out of her rapidly deteriorating mind.

When a husband comes to court and is put in prison, the prison doctor or psychiatrist will often, if he sees that the man is sick, try to have him put into a mental hospital for treatment, as prison is of no therapeutic value. However, the prison psychiatrist will run up against a major snag.

Mental hospitals are geared to treating the mentally ill, but the majority of the husbands have a 'personality problem'. In other words, there is nothing organically wrong with their minds, but their personality needs re-educating. To cure a man who is suffering from a recognized mental illness such as schizophrenia is a complicated but not necessarily impossible task. But to cure a man with a long-term personality disorder will take years and cost an enormous amount of money.

So far our society has made almost no provision for the people we term 'psychopaths'. Given that most mental hospitals are hopelessly overcrowded and understaffed it is not surprising that they usually refuse to take on a man who is not mentally ill, but is liable to be intractable, disruptive and dangerous. The hospital usually reports that there is nothing mentally wrong with him and sends him home.

Most psychiatrists are men, most are middle class and wealthy. In order to train as a psychiatrist they have to spend years studying and inevitably they tend to become buried deeper and deeper in theory and more and more remote from the problems of a battered woman in a working-class home. When faced with a weeping woman complaining of violence from her husband, the psychiatrist's training is likely to blind him to her real needs and reinforce in him the simple notions that a woman's place is in the home with her husband, that even if he is violent that only shows his need for her, and that if she won't stand by him he will be destroyed. Faced with a woman who has put up with years of battering, the psychiatrist is induced to blame her. He doesn't understand the social conditions that make it impossible for her to escape. I have often had psychiatrists say to me in puzzled tones, 'She must have liked it to have stayed for so many years.' It is hard for these men to understand the economic and social dependence women have on men, because they have money in their pockets to buy a roof wherever they choose, and they've been brought up as men to act independently and make decisions. They really cannot imagine how financially and psychologically difficult it is for a mother with children to strike out on her own and find accommodation and money to live on.

Doctors

Very often the first person a battered woman goes to see is her doctor, and he is the first person to ignore the evidence in front of his eyes.

Marie tells me that when she showed a fresh set of bruises to her doctor he laughed and said, 'Call that a beating! Go away and don't waste my time.' This is a fairly typical attitude. The doctor does not want to make a note of the injuries because it means swearing affidavits for courts, which takes time. He is middle class and has been brought up to believe that the working class cannot communicate verbally and always resort to fists and that this is quite acceptable. Therefore he is not sympathetic to battered women who clutter up his clinic and he hands out bigger and bigger doses of tranquillizers.

I think all doctors should be obliged to notify a health visitor at the first sign of bruises on either a mother or child so that she can visit the family and take the necessary action. I doubt that the doctors would bother, because it would take a radical change in attitude to get them to accept that women have a right not to be beaten, and, as the doctors rarely see the middle-class wife who is battered because she hides behind her front door, they assume the myth that battering is a working-class syndrome which, like poverty and disease, will always be with us.

Marriage Guidance

If you shop at Habitat and cook *à la* Elizabeth David and your marriage is going gently wrong then Marriage Guidance will probably suit your needs.

You can discuss 'where it all went wrong', secure in the

knowledge that your councillor will have gone to the same kind of school as you attended and the same kind of dances and probably sold out to the highest bidder. You can also console yourself with the knowledge that 'your case' will be discussed with fervour at tea-tables and coffee-mornings in the areas advertised by Roy Brooks.

If a woman comes to see us and wants to try Marriage Guidance we are always told that there is a waiting list, however desperate she may be.

None of the mothers who have come to Women's Aid found Marriage Guidance any help at all. They didn't understand most of what was said to them and usually found that the councillor was sitting behind her desk with her fingers interlocked, breathing in-phrases like 'marriage is a fit' and relapsing into meaningful silences.

If a wife who left her home town to live with us wanted to attend the same Marriage Guidance centre as her husband so they could at least share the benefit of the experience, she would be told that it's against the rules. Each must go to the office nearest to where they are living.

How Marriage Guidance, with its £300,000 subsidies from the government, has managed to avoid the problem of battered wives for so long baffles me. It isn't as though battering is confined to the working classes who don't go to Marriage Guidance. Rather, I see it as a failure of the organization to fulfil its aims of helping and caring with marriages of all types. They have avoided the problem by taking a comfortable well-heeled position behind their desks and being politely useless whenever it comes up.

The people who benefit most from Marriage Guidance are, I think, those who become councillors. For them it offers instant therapy under the guise of helping others, and under the motherly wing of a tutor it gives them a chance to absorb a bewildering vocabulary of psychiatric jargon suitable for impressing their friends and entertaining at parties.

Marriage Guidance needs guidance itself – towards a role where it can really help people with genuine needs, and away from its present character as the ineffectual illegitimate offspring of the psychiatric consulting room.

The Family Service Unit has existed as an organization for twenty-five years. It was set up to deal with the 'problem family'. It is a voluntary agency staffed by social workers and helpers and funded by local authorities and voluntary contributions. The following passage was quoted in the Family Service Unit's quarterly journal of winter 1973:

'We feel that it is important to differentiate between sporadic "battering" which can be regarded as part of a normal marriage, particularly in certain cultural groups, and more persistent beating.'

Because of that attitude many women who have come into contact with this organization have been encouraged to remain in dangerous situations – sacrificed to the F S U's belief that the family must be kept together at all costs.

In a case where a woman with a child had been cohabiting with a habitual drunkard who was consistently violent, the F S U officer would come into Women's Aid demanding her return. Even though this woman was going to court to get a non-molestation injunction and an eviction order, the F S U worker insisted that time, love and patience could bring them together again.

I do not expect to get 'sporadically battered' in my marriage; neither does the woman who helps to clean the house, nor my dustman's wife. The three of us fail to understand how F S U can have reached their conclusion.

In another F S U article on baby-battering, they draw the conclusion that battered babies grow into battering parents but insist that the male confines inherited violence to his children, and that any violence that he inflicts upon his wife is her own fault: 'women usually make use of other weapons, e.g. of nagging but they frequently provoke, consciously or unconsciously, a violent response in their husbands, often in order to relieve tensions in the relationships.' In other words, she gets what she deserves. When a reputable organization condones violence in family life as a normal part of marital wear and tear, what chance have the mothers of getting away?

These kinds of remarks are usually made by case-workers who

have never been on the other end of a punch or a kick. They are never there when the damage is inflicted. They only arrive hours later when the mother has pulled herself together and is coping again.

One F S U worker told a mother who had been beaten over many years that she should consider herself lucky that he beat her because it proved that he still cared about her and was trying to communicate with her. She didn't go to the F S U again.

The Probation Service

The probation officer can play quite a large role in the life of a battered wife. Often when a woman goes to court to take out a summons she is first referred to the probation office. There they will listen to her case and, though they're not legal experts, they will help her decide her best course of action. If they decide that she does have a case they will help her through the humiliating business of appearing in front of the court and exposing her private life to the scrutiny of those sitting on the bench. If they feel her case cannot succeed they will suggest that she seek legal advice and tell her where to find a solicitor.

When the court decides to put a man on probation for battering his wife, he will also come under the care and control of the probation officer. But, of course, it's not an easy task to control a man who you know is violent towards his family and who may be violent towards you if you thwart him.

Sometimes the only relationship that the husband has with anyone except his wife is with his probation officer, so their relationship can be very constructive.

Most of my experience with the probation officers has been very heartening. Certainly, the old-style officers seem to have a robust and realistic approach to life and a clear view of the people they are there to serve. But I don't feel quite so happy about the young officers who are coming in. They seem to have been painted with the all-embracing 'case-work' brush – the instant psychiatry that too often dilutes action – and they see so many sides of the situation that they are in danger of falling down the hole in the middle.

Fred was a very famous tramp in our area. He was always in

trouble and had been in prison on and off for most of his life. He had been a safe-cracker and, when he described his life's work, his long white fingers would move like restless butterflies and his wrists would become liquid as he mimed the excitement of opening a safe. He did odd jobs for me at Women's Aid and his probation officer would come round to try and track him down. This probation officer was one of the new ones, enthusiastic but naïve. He used to tell me that though neighbours complained about the twelve or so dogs in Fred's grotty flat, he felt that they were the old man's only companions, and how Fred had explained with tears in his eyes about his wife running off with another man.

I didn't like to tell him that Fred was the local dog thief, and that he starved and beat his dogs just as he had starved and beaten his wife.

Nothing in that probation officer's training seemed to have alerted him to the possibility of anyone conning him into believing those wild stories, whereas the old probation officer could smell them a mile off, and, while being just as caring, seemed to retain a sense of humour and reality. Perhaps, given time, the young probation officers will learn, but it would be a pity if, in the race to obtain more and more qualifications, the service loses the kind of officers who react at gut level and goes over to an academic, pseudo-psychiatric approach.

Health Visitors

Wherever she turns for help the battered wife finds every agency blind and deaf or worse, except one. Health visitors are a source of real comfort and help. Time and again wives tell of the help they have sought and of the unhelpful attitudes that were shown to their problems, but they speak highly of their own health visitors.

One of the principal reasons that this organization is such a success is that its women go into the homes. They really roll up their sleeves and are prepared to give any aid they can. Sometimes they will scrub out the house, another time they'll have a cup of tea and just listen. They cuddle the children and know their birthdays. They will often enter a house where the man is known to be violent, even when the doctor and the social worker make a point of standing on the doorstep.

In our early days it was the health visitors who referred their clients to us, often bringing them by car and keeping contact all the while their mothers were with us. Our own social services stayed away but the health visitors came in to see what we were doing and stayed to help.

Their organization is always treated as the Cinderella of the social services, yet it is these dedicated women who really are the backbone of any help the families receive. I would like to see their number increased and their influence extended. Then perhaps a little of it might rub off on some of the high-minded theorists who staff the other agencies and make them so useless to a battered woman.

Chapter 6

The Law – For What It's Worth

I AM not a lawyer, and this chapter cannot contain a comprehensive survey of the law in this field, but I want to set down how the law and its procedures appear to battered women.

So many of the women who come to Women's Aid have been given incorrect or – sometimes worse – incomplete advice by their solicitors. Yet, just as you don't expect to check out that your doctor has given you the right drug, so people take their solicitors' advice in good faith. It horrifies me that solicitors can spread a haze of bad advice and put their clients through weeping misery and still remain respected members of their profession. They are fairly safe from complaints because most people are intimidated at the very thought of solicitors' offices. Knowing this, the solicitors will be so rude and threatening to anyone who complains that they will soon back down.

Very few people know that if they feel they are not getting satisfaction from their solicitors for their divorce they can inspect their files. In London they can go to Somerset House and ask for the Divorce Registry where, provided they show proof of their identity, they can see their own files and check on what is or is not being done.

Out of the 700 women who contact Women's Aid each month over 100 have been given bad legal advice. And the women who come to us are only the tip of the iceberg. I believe that many more thousands of women have been accepting what their solicitors say and putting up with their delays without questioning their probity.

It is quite staggering to discover that so many solicitors just don't know their business. When Nora came in she had been married for seven weeks and been battered three times. The solicitor she'd consulted had told her quite categorically that she would not be able to apply for a divorce because she had not been married for three years. Fortunately I knew from previous experience that she could apply on grounds of exceptional depravity. The beatings, coupled with the fact that she had no idea of her husband's prison or drug record, mean she will probably be free of him within a few months and before she is pregnant and anchored to him.

Jane was beaten persistently by her husband for years. She finally went to a mental hospital to be treated for depression. When she was discharged she was too frightened to go home, so she took a room and she went to a solicitor. The solicitor made no attempt to get her to the divorce court immediately, which he could have done on grounds of persistent cruelty. He said that she would have to wait in her bedsitter for two years in order to provide grounds of irretrievable breakdown of marriage. All that time the husband retained custody of the children and she visited them secretly in the evenings while her husband was visiting his mistresses. The seventeen-year-old son used to baby-sit. When the second son began to stagger whenever he walked, Jane was extremely worried. The doctor saw him, his school knew about it, but they all said that no doubt it was a reaction to the emotional upsets in the family and he'd soon get over it. Jane tried desperately to get him away from the tension of the father's house. She tried the social services and other agencies, but no one offered any help. One evening he became so ill that she took him by taxi to her mother's and there he died in her arms. He had a brain tumour. Soon after the funeral her mother died of the shock.

Jane's now got a petition for persistent cruelty and it looks as though she may get her home and her other children back. When I asked her first solicitor why he hadn't done this eighteen months ago, he said, 'You may do things like that in London, but it's different here.'

Another common pitfall is the solicitor who advises that if the wife leaves the matrimonial home, her husband will be able to sue her for desertion. This is quite wrong: as long as she can show proof that she had to leave because of his unreasonable behaviour it is called 'constructive desertion' and not held against her.

From a solicitor's point of view, battered wives are not good business. The work is often urgent and it takes up a lot of time. A complicated injunction can mean three appearances in court during one week; getting a man committed to prison for breaking an injunction can take four whole days. The fees are small compared with what can be got for commercial work.

Often a woman has to go from solicitor to solicitor trying to get one to take on her case. There are a few disreputable firms who aim to mass-produce divorces by the hundred in order to rake in the fees. This mechanical approach rarely produces a good job for any of their clients, but the complexities of a battered woman's case are beyond the capacity of their sausage-machines.

Before any solicitor will talk to you, he will ask you if you are earning or not. His first concern is getting his money. Unless you are rich you're entitled to legal aid, but many solicitors, to our knowledge, have taken payments from women while knowing that they should instead have legal aid. If you have some money – even if you are scrubbing floors for some minuscule amount – you will get part of the costs paid by legal aid and your divorce, if defended, will cost you about £100. You can pay it off on the never-never at about £6 month. Most of our mothers have no income at all except for supplementary benefits so they qualify for legal aid to pay all the divorce costs. Either way there is a long wait while the application form is sent to the local legal aid office and processed by clerks and committees determined to see that not a penny more of public money is spent than is absolutely necessary.

I know of one solicitor who can get legal aid granted by phone on almost all the cases he thinks urgent enough. This is because he has an unusually close relationship with his local legal aid office, he works for a well-respected firm and he is dogged and determined. In my experience this is a rare combination. Most must wait. The delays can be dangerous and even fatal for a woman and her children.

In one case, a young girl was thrown out of her house and her baby was kept by his dangerous father. The solicitor filled in the forms and sent them off, but we were unable to get legal aid immediately. We knew the baby was in danger so we paid the legal costs out of our own pockets. Even that delay was too long. The husband claimed he meant to hit the dog, and hit the baby instead; the baby is in hospital with brain damage. He could have been saved if we could have got a custody order within hours.

You might have expected that the new neighbourhood law centres would be prepared to help. They were set up by enthusiastic young lawyers in poor districts as places where anybody could come in and discuss their legal troubles in surroundings less imposing than the usual solicitor's office.

When one law centre found that most of their work was matrimonial and they had more than they could cope with, they decided to cut down so that they could continue to operate in the people's interests. They dropped the biggest category, matrimonial cases – so much for caring for the people's needs! Other centres started since have been refusing to take on matrimonial cases right from the start.

When challenged, they say that ninety per cent of divorce work is social work anyway – just passing the buck on. They'll try to justify their policy by giving out that the solicitors in their area give a reasonable service, and that those solicitors would be annoyed if the centres deprived them of this source of work. We've already seen what ordinary solicitors' 'reasonable service' often amounts to, and that's not good enough.

It is said that after famine, unhappy marriages are the greatest cause of human misery. Yet the law centres claim that they are doing more to help by concentrating on housing, social security and criminal cases. They remain well aware that matrimonal cases are a pressing need, for people keep coming to them, but they keep turning them away. If solicitors at law centres won't help these people, who will? The law centres' present policy is an eternal discredit to them. It must be reversed.

For a woman who is being constantly beaten up by her husband, her first need is protection from his beatings. Solicitors are always telling me that the law will protect battered wives if it is properly used and that there are many possible channels of action:

   – prosecution by the police or by the wife under criminal law;

   – a matrimonial summons for cruelty or a separation order in the Magistrates' Court;

   – injunctions in the High Court (or the County Court) pending divorce proceedings.

So where is our problem?

The remedies are there in theory, but in practice none of them can give any peace of mind to a woman who has been beaten by her husband, for they only aggravate his violence and they don't give her any form of protection.

Criminal Prosecution

The Home Office has declared that the law is the same for assaults between husband and wife as for any other assault. But, as we've seen, there is a wide gap between what the law says and what the police will actually do. Even if the police are willing to prosecute, the wife will often ask them not to charge her husband because, without refuge, she and her children will have to live with him up to and during the trial. In this situation she can only lose.

In one case the police did prosecute, but that wasn't much use either, for the man was allowed out on bail for the eighteen months before his case came up for trial. During that time his wife, who had been paralysed down one side by the final assault, was virtually barricaded in the top-floor flat she'd taken while he constantly harassed her. Would the courts let any other criminal but a criminal husband remain out on bail if he continued to threaten the victim whose assault he was charged with?

The Magistrates' Courts

When the police do think some legal action is needed, they usually advise the woman to go to the Magistrates' Court and take out a summons herself. When she goes to the Court, she will probably see first the Clerk of the Court, and he will advise her or send her to the probation officer who will help her fill in a private summons. Once she has done this, she must, unless she can find refuge, go home and wait for the summons to be served on her husband, and even then carry on sharing his bed and breakfast-table. Few can stand the strain and they usually cancel the summons before the case is due to be heard.

If she does stick it out all the way to the court, her fate will rest with the magistrate, usually a lay person who has achieved some sort of public distinction like being a local councillor or a woman who's married a local dignitary. The magistrate will listen to the evidence concerning the assault and then deliver judgment. As it's taken six to twelve weeks to get the case to court the woman will be showing no signs of the damage that began it all. Perhaps this goes some way to explaining the derisory sentences that tend to be passed for wife-battering. For two assaults, an attempted strangulation and a severe blow to the head, a husband was bound over and fined £25 for the first and put on three years' probation for the second. In the following weeks he forced his wife to make up the £25 out of the housekeeping. 'Binding over' simply means that the assault has been noted and that if it happens again the magistrate may take sterner measures. Probation means a visit once a week to the probation officer. All in all a trip to the Magistrates' Court is unlikely to make life any safer for a battered wife.

She must also go to the Magistrates' Court if she needs a separation order from her husband. This may be the initial step towards getting a divorce. It is also an essential passport to maintenance, but magistrates are often unwilling to grant a separation order unless the wife has found somewhere to live. They say that if she is still living with her husband, her situation can't be as bad as she claims. Many magistrates have little knowledge of the perpetual housing crisis and live in large comfortable houses themselves. Sometimes a more enlightened magistrate may allow a separation order even when the wife is still living at home, with the stipulation that they must lead separate lives. For a battered woman this solution is totally unrealistic. Unfortunately, however dreadful the case, magistrates have no power to evict the husband. Many women are directed to the Magistrates' Courts by the police, social workers and other agencies when they would be far better off with an injunction which can at least order the man to vacate the house.

Injunctions

This legal procedure can be quick and it can be tailored to suit each individual case – for these reasons it is the most useful to a battered woman. In London, applications for injunctions of this kind are heard in the Family Division of the Divorce Registry; in the rest of the country they are heard in the local Divorce County Courts.

An injunction is a court order which can describe exactly the kind of behaviour that the wife wants stopped – molesting or assaulting her and the children, loitering near her home or outside the children's schools, telephoning at all hours of the night, or scrawling graffiti over neighbouring walls. It can also order that the wife is to have the custody of the children, maintenance from her husband and the matrimonial home back. So when the court orders the husband and he disobeys, he is in contempt of court and the court can punish him.

The method we use at Women's Aid is to petition for a divorce on the grounds of persistent cruelty, at the same time applying for an injunction. As in the great majority of our cases we have hospital and doctor's evidence, there is little difficulty in getting the injunction granted.

The injunction may not protect her, but at least it's written down somewhere that she has been assaulted and the children are hers. If, when the judge has ordered the husband to vacate the matrimonial home and his wife moves back in with the children, her husband decides to break in and beat her up, the injunction is just like any other piece of paper. There is no point in calling the police to her aid because they cannot arrest on an injunction. The only people who can enforce a High Court injunction are the bailiffs and tipstaffs. They are scarce, they finish at 5.30 and they don't work weekends. It is possible for a judge to ask the police to cooperate in enforcing an injunction, but as it is only a request it is often ignored. I believe the police should be made responsible for enforcing these injunctions. As it is now, the woman has to go back to her solicitor in the morning and he has to apply to the court for another hearing. It all takes a very long time, and meanwhile her husband is marching in and out of the house at will.

Joan took her husband before the High Court eleven times before she finally got him put in prison with a one-year sentence. The first time he broke in the police refused to come as they said there was nothing they could do on a High Court injunction. He beat her up and she came to Women's Aid. After that the poor woman yo-yoed back and forth with her three children using us as a refuge when her husband was around. Eventually she went back and tried to live in the home that the court said was hers when the divorce had been granted. He broke in, beat her up, punctured her ear-drum and raped her at the point of a knife. When she got him back into the High Court, the judge did not appear to have read the previous judges' notes and accepted the husband's story that he dropped in for some urgent papers at 3 a.m. and his wife had refused to let him have them. The judge gave him seven days and told him in effect that he was a naughty boy.

Part of Joan's problem was that whenever she took her husband to court they appeared in front of a different judge, and none of the judges bothered to read the file of her husband's atrocities, which was steadily getting thicker and thicker.

She gave up trying to live in 'her' home and moved in with us. Her husband broke our windows, screamed and raged outside the house, pestered the school and tried to snatch the children. We took him back to court and this time saw the same judge twice. He did read the case and was appalled enough to put him inside for a year. It was too late for Joan to claim her council house, though – the rent arrears had mounted up and the council had taken it back.

Anne's husband split her skull open, and, when she went back to the home the court said was hers, he broke in and kneed her so badly she haemorrhaged inside. She's got her divorce, but her husband will always be after her, so she's had to go into hiding. She won't live for long because her kidneys were damaged by all his kickings.

Even the barristers know that an injunction is useless against an angry and violent man. A frightened woman can get no comfort from knowing that she has enlisted the power of the courts, for if the man is still at large to do as he pleases, a piece of paper from the court can never stop him.

When you see how little the courts usually help a beaten woman, you might wonder why she bothers to go to law in the first place. Even if she would prefer just to hide from her husband for life and forget about legalizing her escape, there are strong pressures on her to go to law. If she needs maintenance money from him, she must act through a solicitor; if she needs money from social security she must prove that she's been to a solicitor and started legal proceedings. Once she goes to a solicitor the whole machine starts to roll, dragging her with it.

Going to court is quite an ordeal. The High Court in the Strand is as awe-inspiring as it sounds. It is a massive crenellated building with white towers and spires outside and a huge arched hall inside. The place is honeycombed with narrow corridors that run off the central hall to the small courtrooms. Everywhere ant-like uniformed figures bustle around. Barristers stride along in their black flapping gowns and wrinkled white wigs, best-suited solicitors scurry in their wake, blue-suited ushers look officious. The people waiting in little knots look shabby and out of place in this impersonal palace of justice.

If the case is to be heard in the morning we have to be there by 10. Waiting to meet the solicitor is always an anxious time because if the husband has been told to attend the court too, it will be the first time that his wife has had to face him since she ran away.

If you manage to avoid meeting him before, you usually find him crouched on the hard little benches that line the ill-lit, crowded corridor outside the courtroom. There, knee to knee and face to face, the couple must wait, sometimes for hours, before they are called into court.

My first time was with Lesley. Pat had come along to hold her other hand and together we had to hold Lesley upright because she was in such a state of fear at the prospect of seeing her husband. He had a terrible reputation, and on the night she had left him, he'd gone to see her friends with a gang and broken into the house. The gang beat up the old couple upstairs and their two sons. It took ten policemen to get them out, and though he was charged he was released on bail. Now we were in court to ask for an injunction to give her custody of the three children, maintenance while her divorce petition went through and a non-molestation order to keep him from carrying out his threat to kill her.

Waiting to go into the courtroom, we were all frightened. The solicitor and the barrister were quite unperturbed, and the barrister gave the impression that Lesley was making an unnecessary fuss. We were due in court mid-morning, so we settled down on the little benches to wait, morosely contemplating the other silent people waiting, and gazing at the stained walls.

The tedium and the peace were disturbed by the arrival of Lesley's husband and his henchmen. Then began a cat-and-mouse shuffle as we moved round the narrow corridors trying to prevent him upsetting Lesley even more. By the time it was our turn Lesley was speechless with fright and we half carried her between us into the court.

The judge glanced at us all and seemed unimpressed. He looked at the affidavits on his desk, scowled, and then a rapid crossfire of conversation began between him and the two barristers. We were not any part of the proceedings. The longest argument was about the costs, with both barristers bobbing up and down and protesting volubly. We had no idea of the outcome until we got outside and our barrister said we had got everything we wanted. We were very pleased, but much more preoccupied with the problem of getting out of the building without the husband and his gang catching us. They lurked and we dodged, until after rushing into lavatories and dashing down long corridors, we slipped out of a back entrance and away.

It all seemed a very furtive and irrelevant piece of theatre. People's whole lives are changed in a few minutes in an uncaring, unfeeling climate. While we were there a young woman came screaming out of the court. Her barrister was trying to pull her into a side corridor, but she threw herself on the floor, writhing, completely out of control in her grief. Her dress rose up her legs and round her waist. Not one of the crowd assembled outside the court reacted with compassion or even with interest. She shrieked in high, jagged sounds, 'My baby, they've taken my baby!' Faces tightened and all the barristers and solicitors turned their backs briskly and went on talking. Her barrister and solicitor were bending over her, telling her to pull herself together. We went over to her. She was a foster mother who had taken care of a child for eight years and was losing him to the natural mother.

The High Court, with its gloom and impersonality, seems to ignore human misery at the same time as intensifying it. The uniforms forbid people to break down and express emotions. The hushed, bustling system ensures that everything is kept as clean and hygenic as possible. When you leave it's like walking out of a morgue. And you haven't had a chance to say what you want – you've been processed like a sausage. Even if the court has found in your favour, if you're a battered wife, you'll soon find you're no better off.

As husbands can terrorize their wives and families, they usually end up in possession of whatever they want to claim – children, home and income. Without protection, which we've seen the law does not give, custody of the children and accommodation provide a dilemma for his wife. Often possession of the children depends on possession of the home, and having the home on having the children.

In custody cases possession is nine tenths of the law. Even in cases where the mother does have custody, if the husband chooses to snatch the child, it is a very long business to get the child back.

Margaret and her baby son, Jonathan, were brought to us by a probation officer who'd been so worried for their lives that she'd come up from Slough to deposit them on our doorstep. Margaret was very young (eighteen). She'd married because she was unhappy at home but the man she married in a hurry turned out to be very dangerous, with a criminal record.

The probation officer called for Margaret at Women's Aid one day and said her husband was now extremely repentant and would she come with her to her office because he said he had a caravan to live in and this would completely alter their way of life. Margaret was persuaded and off they went. She came back a few hours later. He had joined them in the office, grabbed the baby and run out to his car and disappeared. Margaret was desperate. He had never looked after the child and didn't much like him, and she had no idea where they were.

I felt hopeful because Margaret already had a custody order and I thought we would only have to notify the police and they would rush out and rescue the small boy. Not so. We would have to contact our solicitor and go into the High Court and get an order commanding the husband to return the child. Fortunately for us we had a marvellous solicitor who always dropped everything to help us when we had cases of this kind. He took the matter into court the next day and asked the judge to have the child found and returned to the mother. He had to ask the judge permission to give the matter publicity too, and the judge agreed and said the child was to be returned by the next day or a warrant would go out.

Somewhat relieved, Margaret and I left the court. She had her picture taken for the newspapers and a description of the father and child went out. Our old friends, *The World at One*, who helped us whenever we asked, had us in to talk about Jonathan on the radio and we asked people to notify our local police station if they saw him or his father.

Margaret spent another sleepless night and we went back to court for the warrant. The case came up before a different judge, who refused to issue a warrant, saying that we would have to wait until the end of the week in case the husband had not seen the publicity. Margaret was distraught. We went back to Women's Aid and prayed someone would find the baby soon. At the end of the week we went back to court and yet another judge made an order for the husband to return the child to the mother. We thought that now this order had been made we could sit back while the police leaped into their Panda cars and looked for Jonathan. Wrong again. Only the tipstaffs and bailiffs were responsible for finding the child. It was Friday and they don't work weekends. We resolved to find the child ourselves.

The only clue we had was the fact that Margaret's husband was very friendly with some gypsies living somewhere down the M4. We found the site and called the inquiry agent who was to serve the order to return the child. Pat (hugely pregnant) and Lucy climbed into the inquiry agent's car and set off.

When they arrived, Margaret, who had to accompany them so that she could identify her husband, was lying on the floor taking occasional peeks over the back seat. If this sounds melodramatic, you should know that this man tended to go blind with rage and run amok with a meat cleaver – he had once bitten off a man's nose in a fight. In the tension of arriving at the site, Margaret somehow didn't get the right man. She pointed in the direction of a large youth strolling around the site minding his own business. The intrepid inquiry agent leapt out of the car, approached the youth and pressed the order into his hands. The youth shouted and within a few moments the car was surrounded by a pack of gypsies led by the mother of the lad, who was also the Queen of the encampment. Now I had foreseen the possibility of trouble and had asked the police to cooperate, pointing out that gypsies don't like this sort of thing. Luckily that particular constabulary turned out to be unusually helpful.

The mother was hurling abuse, the rest of the gypsies were rocking the car, when down the road came a policeman on a push-bike.

'Here comes the fucking cavalry,' shouted the Queen and, with that, several of the men let off a salvo of bullets into the air.

'I think', said the policeman, 'you had better leave now.' We did, with the policeman peddling furiously behind us.

A little exhausted by the whole episode we sat down for another council of war. Margaret was quite convinced that the baby had been there, and the father. We contacted the police again and they pointed out they could not arrest him even if they did find him, but they would see what they could do.

A few days later, about 4 in the afternoon, the police phoned us and said they had him in the police station on another charge and if we rushed down they would try to get him to hand over the baby.

This time Lucy, Margaret and myself got into my Ami 8 and dashed off down the M4. When we pulled up at the police station we saw a white Mercedes full of large men sitting outside. Those, Margaret told us, were her husband's friends.

We went inside and the policeman took Margaret and me into the interview room. Margaret's husband sat with Jonathan in his arms. He must have weighed about 20 st. Both of them were filthy. Jonathan turned his face away from his mother and wouldn't look at her. I had told Margaret not to make any gestures to antagonize her husband, and she gripped her elbows tightly with her hands.

The policeman talked softly to him, saying that they could keep him overnight on the charge they had and it would go better with him if he was not in contempt of court for withholding the child. Then I started to talk to him and after about half an hour Jonathan suddenly decided to get off his father's knee and went over to Margaret, buried his face in her lap and started crying. She picked him up and the policeman said to the father, 'Let them go now. The baby needs a doctor.'

We left hurriedly and the policeman at the door said, 'I'll hold him for about ten minutes. Get away as fast as you can.'

Ami 8s are marvellous cars but they are not built for speed. We chugged up the road expecting the Mercedes to overtake us at any moment, but mercifully it never did. Margaret examined Jonathan, who had awful rashes and ear trouble. We bought a bottle of wine to celebrate his homecoming. It took weeks before Jonathan stopped screaming every time Margaret moved, and months before he would let her out of his sight.

When we telephoned the police to thank them, they said how lucky Margaret was to have that sort of publicity, for they had cases of husbands who disappeared with the children and the mothers never found them.

Sometimes mothers and children are separated because the mother is forced to leave home without them. If, before she comes to us, she's never told anyone about her husband's brutalities, her husband can gain everybody's sympathy. After all, he's given up his work to care for the children when his wife had picked up and left them, hasn't he? It must therefore be his wife's fault. The aggrieved husband sits in the family home with the children; the desperate wife has to apply to the courts for custody, which can take months, and she has little chance of getting it if she can't provide a home for her children.

Time and time again a judge will grant a divorce on the grounds of the most horrifying cruelty and then turn round and give the husband access to his children.

When Isabel was granted a divorce her solicitor failed to make it clear that one of the little girls had been savagely beaten by the husband. The judge gave him access once a week and we had to watch the two little girls kicking and screaming their way down the garden path to spend the day with their father. I decided that this was just not good enough and moved the mother to a secret address and insisted that the solicitor returned to court. This he did, but, in spite of the mother's evidence, the judge still insisted that the father should have access, though this time he did say it should be in the company of a social worker. That sounded much safer for the children, but it's almost impossible to find a social worker who wants to spend Saturday or Sunday afternoon with a violent man and his children.

One of the girls of that family, aged seven, wrote:

I am here because my dad kept hitting my mum and he has hit me before but not never hit my sister because he likes my sister best. I think he beats my mum up every weekend when he comes in from work.

She still had to see her father. No one consulted *her* about her preferences.

A father's right to access can also be a right to manipulate, as this eleven-year-old found out:

I am here because my mum has been battered by my dad for nearly twelve years. I came to Women's Aid on 17 May 1973 after staying in a home for three days in Liverpool Street. It has been the first time my mum has run away from my dad. When I first came here I didn't like it but after a week I got used to it and now I like it very much.

When my mum got beaten by my dad I got very nervous and ran around to my friend and phoned for the police. When the police came they said they couldn't do anything about it and she was to go to court about it. When my mum and dad had arguments it broke into a fight and then my three sisters would wake up and start to cry and my dad would shout at them and tell them to shut up. Once my dad caught my mum on the chair and nearly strangled her. I tried to pull him off but he jumped on me and started to hit me around my body with both his hands.

I go to see dad every Saturday with my three sisters. One Saturday I went on my own and he said, 'Next week bring the other three and you can stay here for a week or two and let Mummy worry.' But I did not bring them and he said, 'Next time bring them and you won't see Mummy any more.' And then he said, 'Keep saying to Mummy that you want to go home.' I never do and I have not seen him any more.

The law still assumes that *any* father has a right to have access to his children. Solicitors insist to us that there has to be 'a very good reason' for the wife to refuse access. If these wives don't have very good reasons, then who has?

I feel that if a man beats his wife and children to such an extent that the court sees fit to grant the wife a divorce on the grounds of exceptional cruelty then he has forfeited all rights to his home and family unless and until he has taken treatment that makes it safe for the family to allow him back into their lives.

As it is I see many children forced into the company of men who have ill-treated and tormented them, because basically British law sees women and children as possessions or assets, and will not consider what the human element is when considering what rights a violent man should have over his wife and children.

There is often a terrible bitterness over the splitting up of property and homes after a divorce. If the grounds for the divorce were cruelty you can be sure the husband will make things as difficult as possible. He usually refuses to pay maintenance, but if the mother goes to social security and really insists, they will pay her supplementary benefits and make themselves responsible for collecting the maintenance money from him.

If the mother is middle class the position can be very grim. She probably has big overheads to keep up and, if he refuses and procrastinates, she will soon find herself in trouble with everybody. The children's school fees, the mortgage (social security will only pay the interest on a mortgage), the rates – it quickly becomes a nightmare.

If a battered mother is given her matrimonial home and manages to live in it – in spite of harassment from her ex-husband – she will only be allowed to stay in it until the children grow up and leave. Then her ex-husband can apply to the court and have the house sold. The wife must then move out of the house that she has lived in for many years and find somewhere else to live. She will get at most fifty per cent of the profit after the mortgage is paid. She's too old to get a mortgage for another home and she usually has to leave the district, so she loses her friends and her roots. I think that if a divorce is granted on grounds of cruelty, the house should be given to the wife for her lifetime.

The financial hearing takes place after the divorce and then the whole business is treated like an ordinary parting of the ways where neither side is to blame. It is ludicrous to pretend that a woman who has been savagely beaten and perhaps crippled by violence should be treated as though she is amicably leaving her husband by mutual agreement, with no blame attaching to either side. It may help to make ordinary divorces less painful, and that's fine, but a divorce which is caused by the husband's savaging of the wife is not ordinary. He is to blame, and she should be compensated by sharing out the assets in her favour. At the moment the law makes no provision for this – even the new Criminal Injuries Compensation laws give the right to compensation to anyone who has been assaulted *except* a wife assaulted by her husband. I think this should be amended to include anyone who has been assaulted, and that a battered wife divorcing her tormentor should have a claim against him.

Some changes in the present system would make the country a safer place for the wife and children of the man who is fast with his fists. Legal aid must be speeded up, and the police must be required by law to enforce injunctions. This would at least give the wife a chance to live in peace once she's been to the courts.

It's a matter of enforcing the law rather than substantially changing it. In a democratic society laws are made for reasonable men. To protect our mothers against their violent husbands by law would require very tough laws – so tough that they would penalize the men who need no more than a reminder that resorting to bullying is not acceptable. The law is only as strong as the will to enforce it and the will to obey it. Between the law with its guardians and practitioners on the one hand, and asocial, violent husbands on the other, thousands of women and children are suffering.

I don't believe that the court is the proper place to resolve the problems of battered wives. Their husbands are outside the law: they have been imprinted with violence from childhood, so that violence is part of their normal behaviour. All the legislating and punishment in the world will not change their methods of expressing their frustrations.

I think the most practical use of the law is for it to ensure that in every case of extreme violence the man is shut off from further contact with his wife and children. He must be remanded for psychiatrists' reports, and if they say he has a personality disorder – a behaviour problem – he must not be abandoned by psychiatry and the law and allowed to go free to persecute his family again. He must be detained and given treatment for however long it takes for him to become safe. Prison is no alternative to effective psychiatry, but if psychiatry can't cope, then prison for one man is better than suffering for his whole family, which is what usually happens now.

Chapter 7

Where Do We Go From Here?

WOMEN'S Aid has come a long way from four small rooms and an outside bog, but the organization of Women's Aid has always remained very simple. We now have five large houses and over 250 women and children, but we still work by the same kind of house rules that we began with three years ago.

No one but the mothers taking refuge in the house may answer the telephone or sit behind the small desk and run the open diary. This does not mean that anyone who telephones for one of the volunteers may not speak to them but it is a safeguard to stop well-meaning do-gooders from coming in and taking over the source of power and information. The diary records all the daily happenings at Women's Aid and the cases who phone in. For a new mother who has been down-trodden and systematically destroyed for years, the fact that she is required to run the office gives her back a belief in her own ability and worth.

All letters that come into Women's Aid are opened at about 10 o'clock each morning in the general sitting-room which serves as an office and everyone who's there can read them. Then the letters are put on a clipboard and remain open to everyone. This is important because it helps to keep everyone in the community a part of the whole and to ensure that no one corners power by locking up a vast amount of information in their head.

All financial decisions are made at house meetings and therefore all expenditure is known to everyone and agreed. None of the members of the limited company that form the charity can ever be paid. This seems to me to be a sensible safeguard against career-minded professionals. The only salaries go to the playgroup leader and assistant, some other helpers for the children, the national coordinator and the secretary, and fees are paid to the solicitor and the accountant. This leaves most of the donations we get to go direct to the mothers and children.

House meetings are held every week, but so far we have never had to hold a committee meeting and pass out minutes and agendas, and I hope we never shall. Of course we've formed the required body to comply with the Charity Commissioners and they will sit once a year as required along with David, our long-suffering solicitor, but this formality is irrelevant as far as life in the house is concerned. There the decision-making remains the same: one vote for each person and if there is anyone to be asked to leave, those of us who come from outside have no say and the house vote must be unanimous.

Anyone can ask for a house meeting if something contentious arises. It could be an incident of violence between two women and there the rule is that any adult who raises a hand to another adult must leave the community. It is understood that everyone there is escaping from violence and it would be damaging to experience it in the community. It has only happened twice in two years though. The most often-discussed point is who is leaving the washing up.

We have the accountant, the solicitor, and the national co-ordinator whose job is to tour the country visiting groups that are starting up. It seems to me that this is about all we need at this time, and the set-up has been rounded off by taking on a secretary/bookkeeper to sort out the piles of valuable information that are coming in from all over the world. We have visits every week from the health visitors and the local medical officer, Dr Prothero, who comes in every fortnight to see everyone. We also have various students from polytechnics doing their training with us.

This seems to me to be a fairly unstructured but sound system of administering Women's Aid. I am adamant that we will always remain loosely based on this kind of free structure. The main reason why Women's Aid has grown so fast is because the atmosphere is right; it is run by battered women for battered women.

One of the bitter lessons for the charities of our time must be the experience of Shelter. Not many months ago a mother from Ealing came to me in tears. She had a good husband and five children and they were to be evicted from their home for non-payment of rent. The property was the sort used by the councils to house families temporarily, but they had been there five years. It was the usual sort of appalling place with no hot water, no bath, and damp, peeling walls. The social services had said that unless the family were able to find alternative accommodation for themselves and their five children they would take all five children into care.

I telephoned the social worker who insisted they must act because the husband had been in and out of hospital for the last two years and now owed £700 in rent. I said it would cost £150 a week to keep the children in care. This was treated as irrelevant. I had little time as the bailiff was due the next day, so I telephoned Shelter's homeless family unit. Now Shelter is a charity that began as a dynamic force, feared by complacent bureaucrats, and able to act swiftly and effectively in cases like this one. But, in a few years, Shelter has bogged down in its own bureaucracy. When I told them of this family's desperate plight, they didn't say they'd get straight round to the borough housing department, they didn't even say they'd phone. They said they would write a letter. Sadly, the days have gone when they would get out of their office, go down and see the people concerned and get something done. In this case, the borough was directly contravening a Ministry circular that stated that families should be kept together at all costs, but Shelter let it pass.

It goes without saying that Women's Aid could never have got far without money. Money was, is and always will be the biggest problem. A lot has come in small donations from concerned people, but it's the big companies with money to spare who can make all the difference between survival and collapse to infant charities like us. Yet the spirit in which they give their money has to be right.

It is interesting to contrast the giant construction company Bovis with another big firm that considered helping us. Bovis, under their chairman Neville Vincent, asked what we needed and simply gave it – with no strings. They gave us a £30,000 house as our headquarters and £9,500 to convert and decorate it. This charitable gesture made Women's Aid a going concern. It shows how a large firm with generosity and imagination can have a powerful effect on a social problem.

But another company sent their trust manager to see us in a different spirit. They offered to buy for us a house that belonged to a certain friend of the directors who needed to sell in a hurry. When we looked over the house we realized it would be wrong to move our violent children into its quiet, tree-lined crescent, especially as the house had no garden. It would be hell for both our kids and the neighbours. We said no, but that we were still desperate for a large property where we could house mothers who had been so badly battered that they would need community care for life. The man from the trust left saying he would see what he could do and how much his trust would like to help us.

I should have known better than to believe him. Even as I had been explaining the set-up at Women's Aid I had seen his brow furrow. And alarm had spread across his face as I described the loose structure of the new groups that were spreading across the country. It may have seemed loose to this businessman, but it was working.

We had groups starting up in Basildon, Basingstoke, Birmingham, Blackburn, Blackpool, Brighton, Bristol, Burnley, Coventry, Dublin, Edinburgh, Glasgow, Lancaster, Leeds, Leicester, Liverpool, Brixton, Camden, Hackney, Harringay, Islington, Lewisham, Southwark, Tower Hamlets, Wandsworth, Manchester, Middlesbrough, Newcastle-on-Tyne, Norwich, Nottingham, Rugby, St Albans, Sheffield, Sunderland, Swindon, Surrey, Tunbridge Wells and Worthing. All these had sent representatives down to us and we'd spent hours advising them. Nationally, Women's Aid was developing well. At home things were going soundly too: we were already registered as a charity, we had produced a comprehensive report and the first three editions of a nationally circulated monthly magazine called *Nemesis*. Jack Ashley had raised the question of battered women in Parliament. We had a three-year independent research project under way, in the hands of an experienced psychiatrist – Dr John Gayford from Warlingham Park Hospital. We'd held an informal national conference where all thirty-eight groups had discussed how Women's Aid should develop nationally. And while doing all this, we were caring for hundreds of mothers and children. It worked.

Having followed Shelter's decline carefully I had decided early on that all Women's Aid groups must remain autonomous and responsible to themselves. This way we would avoid the top-heavy, London-based administrative structure which would mean the death of initiative in the out-of-London branches, because they would feel their help and effort were merely supportive. We had decided on a regional structure, where neighbouring groups could share problems, and with national meetings once a quarter so that major policy problems could be thrashed out.

The regional groups broke down into: Yorkshire, Humberside, North West, Midlands, East Anglia, South East, South West, Wales and Scotland. And the big city areas: Greater London, Tyneside and Wearside, Greater Manchester, Merseyside, West Yorkshire, Birmingham, and West Midlands. Some groups like Liverpool were on their feet and away within a matter of months: each group reflected its own attitudes. For example, while Liverpool kept many of our ideas, Birmingham decided to have a wardened hostel.

Travelling round the country and visiting groups, and listening at our conference, I had noticed that we had people from all walks of life and all political convictions. With a loose but friendly structure I believed that they could all work together and avoid the worst of the in-fighting and political intrigue that bedevils so many more closely knit organizations. It seemed to me that Women's Aid knew where it was going, and was well set up to get there.

However, a few days after the departure of the man with the millions to bestow, I received a letter from him which said, among other things, that while he appreciated the warmth and urgency of our method of dealing with the situation he felt we needed a 'proper administrative framework'. It didn't take long to find out who was going to administer this proper administrative framework. I had a telephone call from an assistant director of social services from a neighbouring borough who had an appointment to lunch with the great man himself and was all set to start a proper movement and show us well-meaning amateurs how things ought to be done.

I listened to his lecture and then asked if, while he was waiting to start, he would care to contribute towards the upkeep of some of the families his own social workers had been unable to help and had referred to us. The irony missed him – he just said he was very sorry but, as we were officially *persona non grata*, there was nothing he felt he could do.

After a short, sharp house meeting I telephoned money-bags and told him that if he went ahead and distributed money in such a way as to threaten all we had worked for, we were no longer interested in his money. He could keep it. There was a long silence on the other end.

There was a silence our end too, after I put the phone down and contemplated the empty cash box. It's hard to be pure sometimes.

Structural changes may eventually evolve, but they won't be forced on us. For the moment we are getting on with what we are doing and allowing other groups to do the same in a way that gives everyone time for a natural structure to develop. No doubt some of the groups that have sprung up are only there because wife-battering is a new and trendy issue. In a year's time they will have gone and only the serious, hard-working groups will remain.

Just as Women's Aid will grow in Britain, I believe its influence must spread round the world. Certainly the letters we get show that wife-beating is international, and so is the growing move to stop it. Sheila Bittner from the Legal Aid Bureau, Inc., in Baltimore, U S A, writes:

From a study done at this agency, I have found that a similar project to Women's Aid is needed for the Baltimore metropolitan region. As in Britain, wifebeating is widely practised in the United States. Though legal intervention is the official recourse for these women, in practice it has been found a greatly inadequate and arbitrary system. The women and children of domestic assault cases are largely left unprotected and unaided.

Nikki Nelson writes from United Charities of Chicago: 'As a social worker at a legal agency that many such women turn to, following a physical confrontation with their husbands, I am involved with this problem on a daily basis . . .' and the long letter goes on to ask about our experience.

From other parts of America I have had visits from similarly concerned people. One splendid Women's Liberationist announced that she and her friends had decided to form a 'goon squad' to catch the wife-beaters, strip off their clothes, handcuff them to lamp-posts and tie blue ribbons around their 'dicks'. Our male playgroup assistant left the room hurriedly, and for a moment I had a vision of all the lamp-posts in Hounslow occupied by erring husbands, but we sighed and said life was not that simple.

We had a long discussion with a New York journalist who had been reporting on the wave of family violence from husbands newly returned from Vietnam. She spent a long time talking to women at the centre and found many similarities between their cases and those that she'd seen at home, with the difference that the violence of the Vietnam veterans seemed to die down after a period of time.

Another sociologist from New England said that wife-battering in America had been acceptable because, like England, it was believed that it only happened at the bottom of society – in America that meant among the blacks and Puerto Ricans. This same attitude existed for years about the drug problem until it was suddenly discovered that the sons and daughters of the American middle class were hopelessly hooked. Then a full-scale panic ensued and money was poured into drug rehabilitation centres. Now it was becoming evident that even managers of large corporations beat their wives and diamond-studded daughters of America are worried about their marriageable daughters – you don't know who you can trust nowadays.

From Canada we get a more diffuse picture. They have got some way towards defining and accepting the problem but as Jim McKenzie, from the Crisis Intervention and Suicide-Prevention Centre for Vancouver, says:

Our Home Placement Programme deals with many different kinds of people in various circumstances including wives who have left their husbands. Many times, due to lack of vacancies in our host homes, we have to refer women with children to other agencies . . .

136